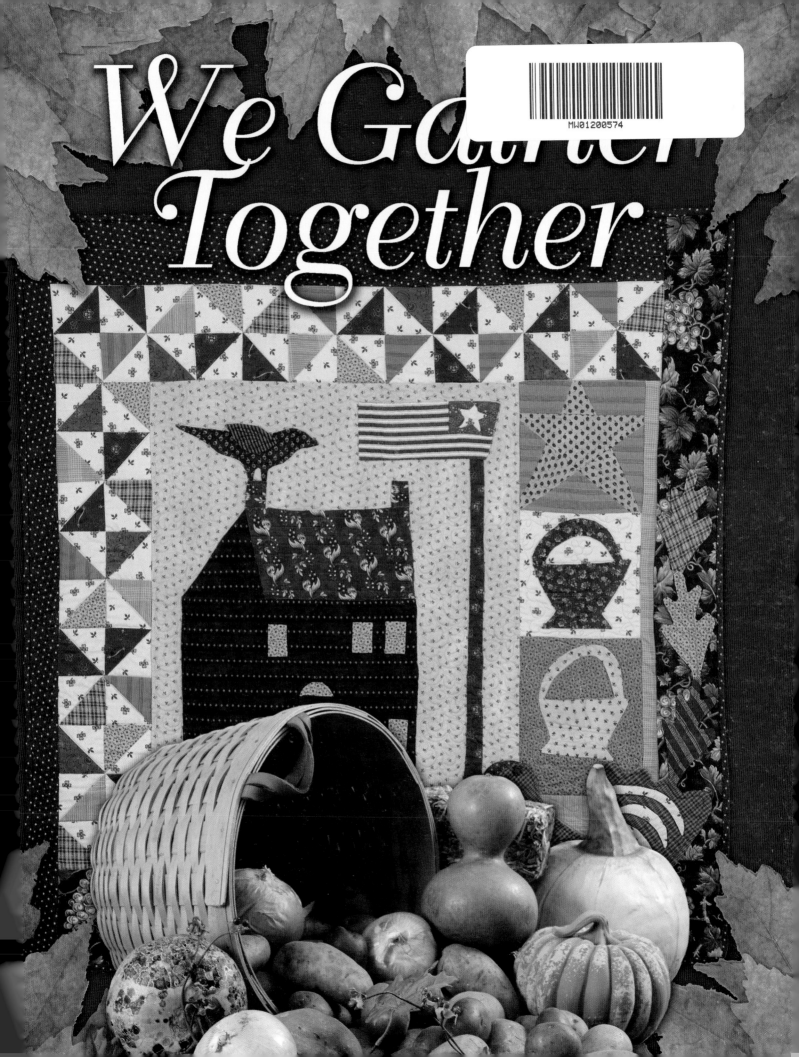

We Gather Together

We Gather Together
A Harvest of Quilts
Author: Jan Patek

Editor: Edie McGinnis
Technical Editor: Christina DeArmond
Designer: Kelly Ludwig
Photography: Aaron T. Leimkuehler
Illustration: Jan Patek
Production assistance by Jo Ann Groves

Published by:
Kansas City Star Books
1729 Grand Blvd.
Kansas City, Missouri, USA 64108

First edition, first printing
ISBN-978-1-933466-68-2
Library of Congress Control Number: 2008928290

Printed in the United States of America by
Walsworth Publishing Co., Marceline, MO

To order copies, call StarInfo at (816) 234-4636 and say
"Books."

✳ **KANSAS CITY STAR BOOKS**

The Quilter's Home Page

www.PickleDish.com

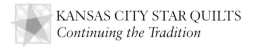

KANSAS CITY STAR QUILTS
Continuing the Tradition

Contents

Introduction

*A*utumn *— Just the word conjures up visions of leaves falling from the trees and crunching under foot.* The nights are cooler and there is a snap to the air. The frost decorating the chrysanthemums warns us that Old Man Winter is getting read to bluster his way to our door. Midwestern farmers have their combines in the fields and are harvesting their crops. Golden kernels of corn spill from the corn picker into wagons. Soybeans are cut and popped from their pods and are soon on their way to market.

Near Peoria, Illinois, pumpkins are harvested. About ninety per cent of the pumpkins raised in the United States, are grown within a 90-mile radius of this Central Illinois city. Most are trucked to the canning factories, shipped to the grocer's shelves then turned into pies, breads and soups. Then there are also those that are used for the Pumpkin Chucking contests where grown men build elaborate machines that cost thousands and thousands of dollars to see who can hurl a pumpkin the farthest.

In times past, harvesting the crops was a tremendous chore and not every farmer had the necessary equipment. Many times folks would get together and help one another bring in the crops. They would go from house to house until all the crops were in. It was the neighborly thing to do.

Early in the morning everyone would arrive at the first farmer's house. The men would go to the fields and the women would begin to cook lunch for their hardworking men. Home-canned green beans, bread and butter pickles, and pickled beets were added to the spread by the women who had already harvested their crops from the gardens they grew. Sweet potatoes, onions and white or red potatoes were retrieved from the root cellars and cooked to add to the feast. Pumpkins and apples made their way into tasty pies for desert.

After the men had eaten, rested a bit and swapped tales, they would go back to work. The tables were cleared and, if the ladies happened to be quilters, out would come the quilting frame. The rest of the day would be devoted to chatting about family events and other matters of importance while quilting on one of the quilts someone had lovingly pieced or appliquéd.

In Colonial Times, harvesting was far more difficult and laborious. Corn was cut by hand and put into shocks. There were no time and labor saving machines such as we know now. But still, helping one another was part and parcel of being a good neighbor. The settlers helped harvest each others fields and the women cooked. One treat made during those years was the forerunner of our pumpkin pie. They would cut off the top of the pumpkin, scoop out the seeds and fill the pumpkin with milk, spices and honey. The pumpkin was then baked in the hot coals of the fire.

The Native Americans had their own way of taking care of their harvest. Much of their food was dried. Buffalo and deer meat was made into jerky. Pemmican (a combination of dried fruits or berries and dried meat and fat) was a staple in their diet. Pumpkins were a valued source of nutrition and long strips of the yellow-orange fruit were roasted over open fires and eaten. The seeds were roasted and used as food and medicine. Longs strips of pumpkin were dried and woven into mats.

Of course, pumpkins have been used for entertaining children and adults at Halloween for years. Hours are spent carving Jack-o-Lanterns for Halloween. Who will make the scariest? Who will make the funniest? Who will make the ugliest Jack-o-Lantern?

As far as my family was concerned, one of the best treats to come out of the pumpkin was the seeds. We washed them, salted them and baked them in the oven at a low temperature. After they were dried, we snacked on them until our mouths were sore from the salt.

Not only do pumpkins make great pies and Jack-o-Lanterns, they make wonderful appliqué elements on quilts and rugs. Combine the pumpkins with some crows or leaves or stars, on some soft homespun backgrounds and you'll get a glimpse of the artistry of Jan Patek.

Jan's quilts are made in a primitive style that suggests warmth and comfort. Choose one of the patterns offered on the following pages and make your own fall quilt to snuggle under and ward off the chill of the cool autumn nights to come. − Edie McGinnis

About the Author

Jan Patek of Jan Patek Quilts began quilting 28 years ago when she quit working to be a stay-at-home mom. With her high energy level and bottomless pit of ideas, she was afraid she would be bored. Dozens of books and patterns later, boredom hasn't been a problem.

Jan began making art quilts to express her creative spirit. She then began to publish patterns to help pay for her fabric fetish. Her first "Snowbound" quilt evolved from a combination of patterns and designs one year when her children requested a Christmas quilt. Her patterns, books and fabric have been big sellers ever since.

Jan Patek and Linda Brannock began designing fabric for United Notions in 1992. They have an extensive line of brushed homespuns and prints under the Moda label. The prints come in a large range of sizes and patterns. The brushed cotton homespuns add texture and co-ordinate with the prints nicely.

Jan's love of family and the creative process have combined to influence her art. Each of her quilts make a statement to which we can all relate. Her "Angel" quilt represents the need for guardian angels. Other work represents the strong bond of family and friends. The quilts are a story of her life, her experiences, and her soul.

To keep up with Jan, check out her Website at www.janpatekquilts.com.

Acknowledgements

Thanks to Helen Williams and Barbara Dunnaway for all the great appliqué work they've done for me over the years. I appreciate Cherie Ralston for being my left brain. My quilts wouldn't look nearly as good without Lori Kukuk's awesome quilting. I wouldn't have nearly enough time to design and make quilts without Shannon Jenkins and, now, Barbara Arnold doing such a great job of handling the office.

Thanks to Aaron Leimkuhler for the lovely photos and Jo Ann Groves for working her magic on them. I want to thank Rita Briner, Quilter's Station in Lee's Summit, Missouri, for lending props for the photo shoot. I appreciate Christina DeArmond for doing such a great job on the technical edit. Thanks also to Kelly Ludwig, my page designer, for making the pages look so great. A special thanks to Doug Weaver, head of Kansas City Star Books and my editor, Edie McGinnis.

General Instructions

Fabric

Whenever possible, use 100% cotton fabric, especially for appliqué. Cotton holds a crease well and allows you to turn under a sharp edge. And it does not fray easily which is necessary for sharp points. Wash all of your fabric before using. Test darks, especially reds, by putting them in with a white rag or washcloth. If the cloth is not white at the end of the wash, find out which fabric bled and rewash, using a cup of vinegar in the rinse water. There is also a product, Retayne, on the market with which we have had good results.

Bias:

The bias of the fabric is the diagonal line across the weave of the fabric. When you cut a square and cut it in half diagonally and then cut strips from this diagonal cut, these strips will be bias strips. They will have more stretch than crosswise or lengthwise strips and mold well around curves.

Bias Binding:

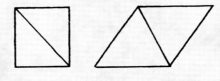
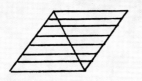
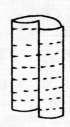

Cut a square in half once on the diagonal. You now have two triangles. With right sides facing, sew along the diagonal. You should now have a piece that looks like a parallelogram. Press the seam open. Draw cutting lines across the parallelogram. I like to use 2 1/2" wide strips for my binding and 1/2" strips for my vines, plus the 1/4" seam allowances. With right sides together, pin the raw edges offsetting them by one width of the binding or vine strip. This will form a tube. Sew together with a 1/4" seam allowance. Press the seam open. Follow the pencil line and cut a continuous strip using scissors. For binding, fold in half and press. I prefer to baste my vines on my quilt, then needle turn the edges. But you could press the seam allowance under before applying to your quilt.

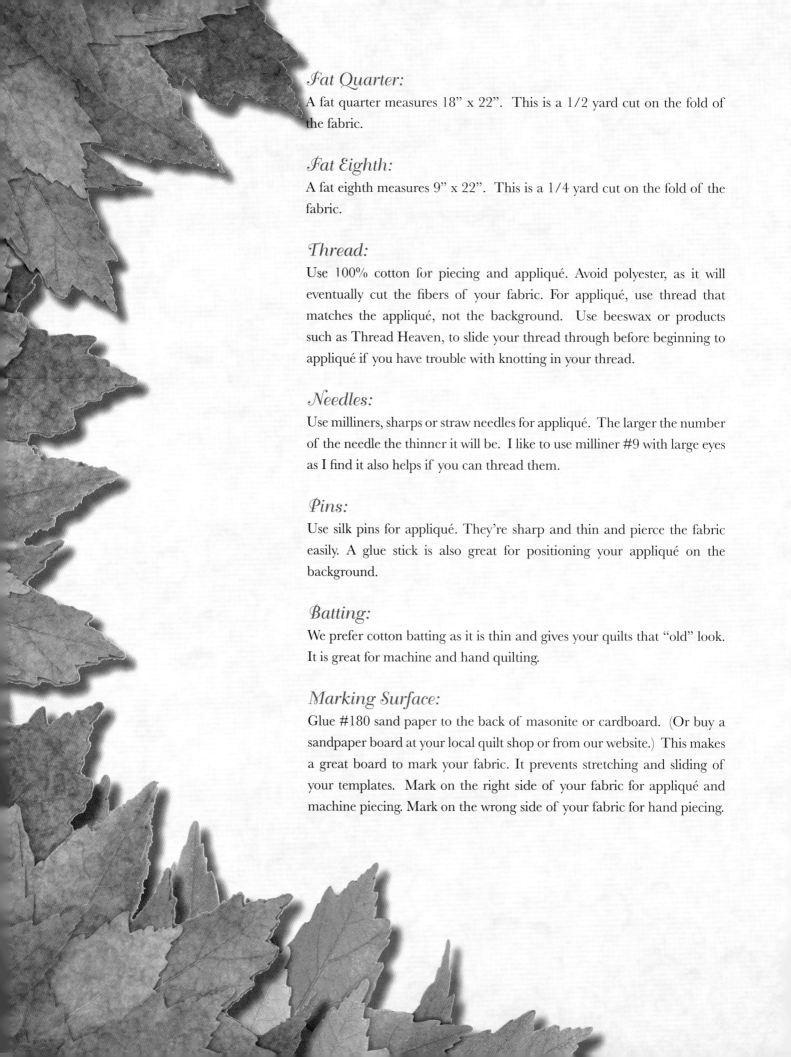

Fat Quarter:

A fat quarter measures 18" x 22". This is a 1/2 yard cut on the fold of the fabric.

Fat Eighth:

A fat eighth measures 9" x 22". This is a 1/4 yard cut on the fold of the fabric.

Thread:

Use 100% cotton for piecing and appliqué. Avoid polyester, as it will eventually cut the fibers of your fabric. For appliqué, use thread that matches the appliqué, not the background. Use beeswax or products such as Thread Heaven, to slide your thread through before beginning to appliqué if you have trouble with knotting in your thread.

Needles:

Use milliners, sharps or straw needles for appliqué. The larger the number of the needle the thinner it will be. I like to use milliner #9 with large eyes as I find it also helps if you can thread them.

Pins:

Use silk pins for appliqué. They're sharp and thin and pierce the fabric easily. A glue stick is also great for positioning your appliqué on the background.

Batting:

We prefer cotton batting as it is thin and gives your quilts that "old" look. It is great for machine and hand quilting.

Marking Surface:

Glue #180 sand paper to the back of masonite or cardboard. (Or buy a sandpaper board at your local quilt shop or from our website.) This makes a great board to mark your fabric. It prevents stretching and sliding of your templates. Mark on the right side of your fabric for appliqué and machine piecing. Mark on the wrong side of your fabric for hand piecing.

Freezer Paper Appliqué:

Draw on the matte side and iron the shiny side to the fabric (iron to the wrong side if you need the pattern reversed). Draw your templates the exact size, do not add seam allowances. Cut out the freezer paper templates. Iron onto right side of fabric and cut out, adding 1/4" seam allowance. If you iron templates onto the wrong side of fabric, your pattern will be reversed. Mark around the templates with colored pencil or chalk and peel off freezer paper. Freezer paper appliqué templates are reusable.

Place the shapes on the background.

Pin, glue stick or baste the shapes into place on the background.

Freezer Paper Templates:

You can also use freezer paper to make templates for piecing. Draw your pattern block on the matte side of the freezer paper. Label all sections of your block. Cut apart and iron the shiny side of the freezer paper to the right side of the fabric, (iron to the wrong side if you need the pattern reversed) allowing enough room to add your 1/4" seam allowance. Use a ruler to add a 1/4" seam allowance to each template. Then either mark the cutting line with a pencil and use scissors or simply cut at the edge of the ruler with a rotary cutter. Freezer paper templates are reusable.

Terminology:

You will need to add a 1/4" seam allowance to templates unless otherwise noted. When we refer to a "scrap," 1/8 yard will be adequate.

(+sa) = add seam allowance

Berries

Making berries or flower centers is a cinch if you follow our easy method.

Trace the circle the required number of times. Cut the circles out. For larger berries, cut the fabric 1/4" larger than your pattern. For very small ones, cut a fabric circle between 1/8 and 1/4" larger than your paper pattern. (I keep my patterns and fabric circles in a bag so I don't lose any.) Make a knot in your thread and do a running stitch around the outer edge of fabric. Place your paper pattern inside and pull the thread until fabric is snugly around your paper berry. Backstitch and cut your thread. Appliqué the berry in place. You can use tweezers to remove the paper if you're making a quilt and don't want the paper left in.

Give Thanks

Size: 26" x 28"

Fabric Requirements

- Background block: 5/8 yard
- Turkey:
- Body: Fat quarter
- Wing: Fat eighth
- Markings: Scraps
- Beard, comb, legs and wattle: Scraps

Pumpkins:

- Fat eighth of 3
- Scraps for middle and center of one
- Scraps for stems
- Letters: Fat eighth of 2 fabrics
- Stop Border: 1/4 yard
- Outer Border: 1/2 yard
- Binding: 5/8 yard
- Corner square: Scrap

Instructions:

Cut an 18 1/2" x 20 1/2" square of background fabric. Make freezer paper templates for all appliqué pieces. Refer to the General Instructions if necessary.

Place the shapes on the background. Pin, glue or baste the shapes into place on the background. Refer to the photo for placement purposes. Appliqué in place.

Borders:

- Cut 2 - 18 1/2" x 1 1/2" inner borders and sew to the top and bottom of the quilt.
- Cut 2 - 22 1/2" x 1 1/2" inner borders and sew to the sides of the quilt.
- Cut 2 - 22 1/2" x 3 1/2" outer borders and sew to the sides of the quilt.
- Cut 1 - 23 1/2" x 3 1/2" outer border. Cut a 3 1/2" square and sew it to the left end of the border piece. Sew to the top of the quilt.
- Cut 1 - 26 1/2" x 3 1/2" outer border and sew to the bottom of the quilt.
- Quilt as desired.
- Sew the star button eye in place.

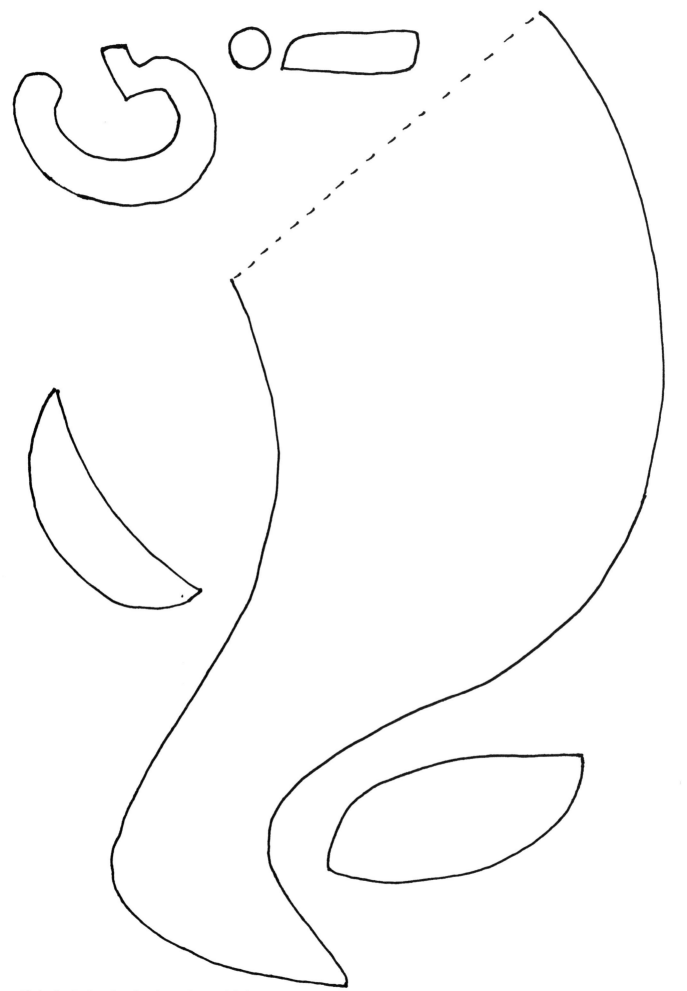

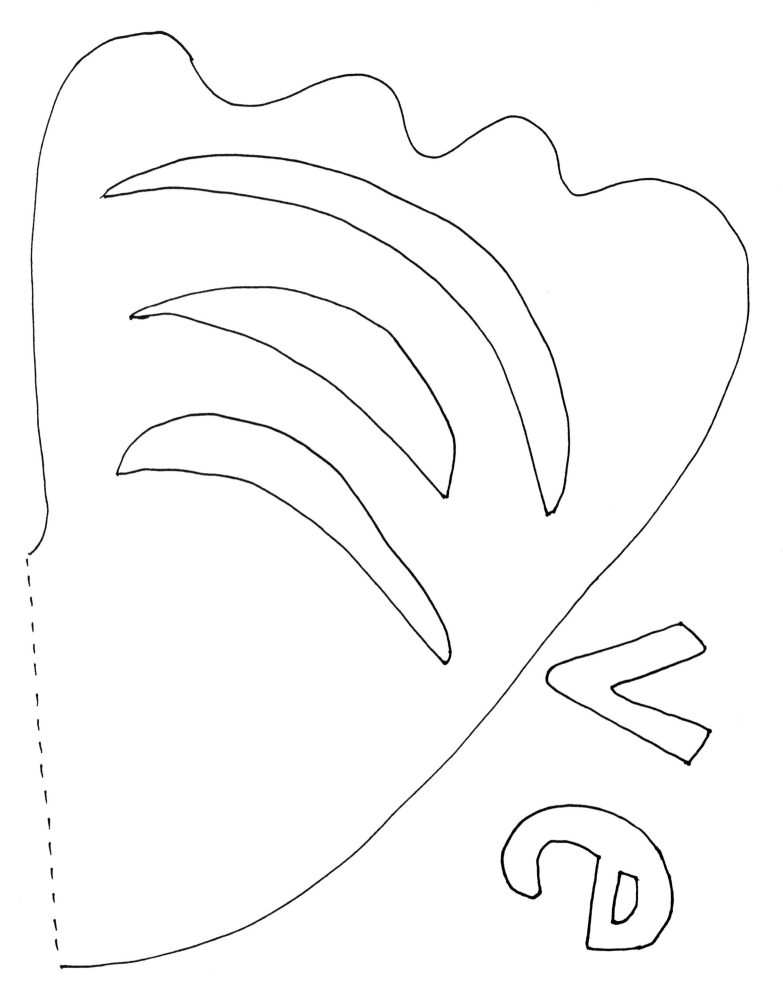

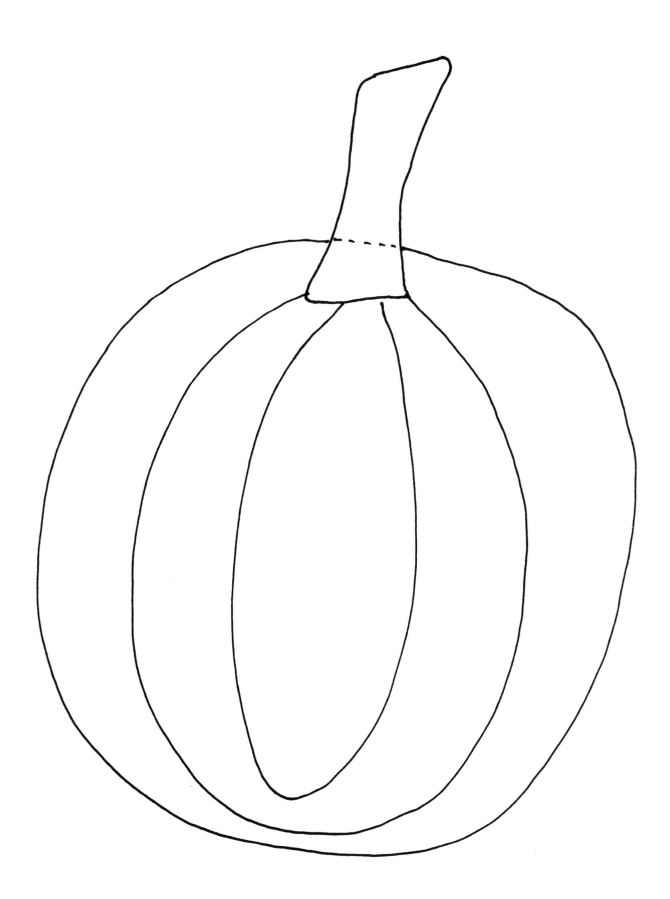

Pumpkin Man

Size: 26" x 38"

Fabric Requirements:

- Background: 5/8 yard
- Pumpkin section and arms: 1 fat eighth for each
- Bat and cat: 1 fat eighth each
- Stem, eyes, nose and mouth of pumpkin: Scraps
- Inner border: 1/4 yard
- Outer border: 1/2 yard
- Binding: 5/8 yard

Instructions:

(all measurements includes seam allowances)

- Cut background block 18 1/2" x 30 1/2"
- Make freezer paper templates of your pumpkin man, stem, bat and cat. (Use the pumpkin stem that's on page 15.) Refer to the General Instructions for directions if necessary.

Borders:

- Cut two 18 1/2" x 1 1/2" stop borders and sew to top and bottom.
- Cut two 32 1/2" x 1 1/2" stop borders and sew to sides.
- Cut two 32 1/2" x 3 1/2" outer borders and sew to sides.
- Cut two 26 1/2" x 3 1/2" outer borders and sew to top and bottom.

Quilt as desired. (We used linen floss for large, even primitive stitches. Lay the buttons on the center pumpkin section and draw a light circle around them with a pencil. Use the pencil lines to quilt the circles)

Sew the buttons to the quilt.

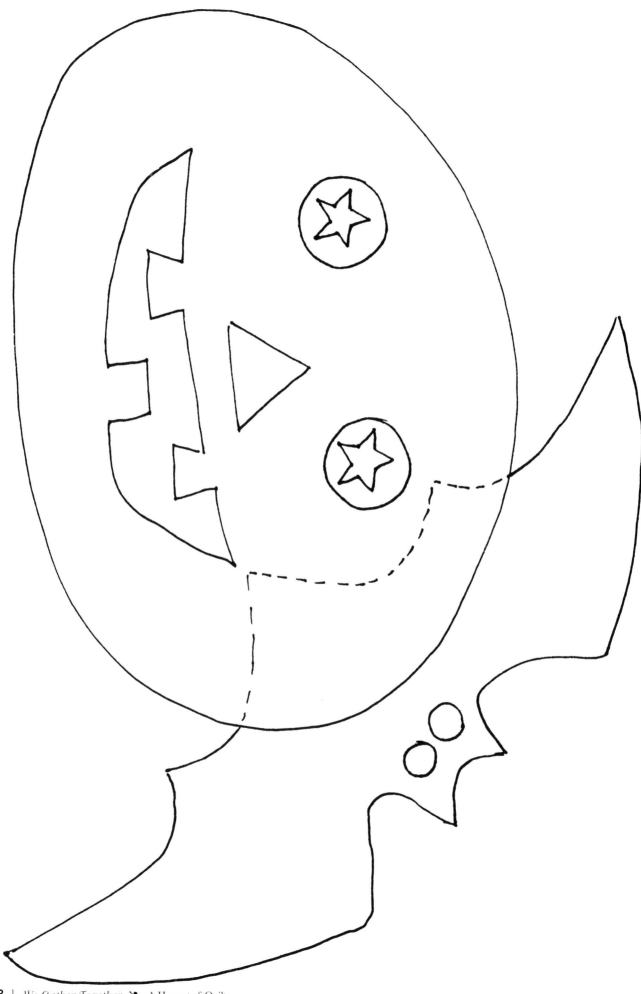

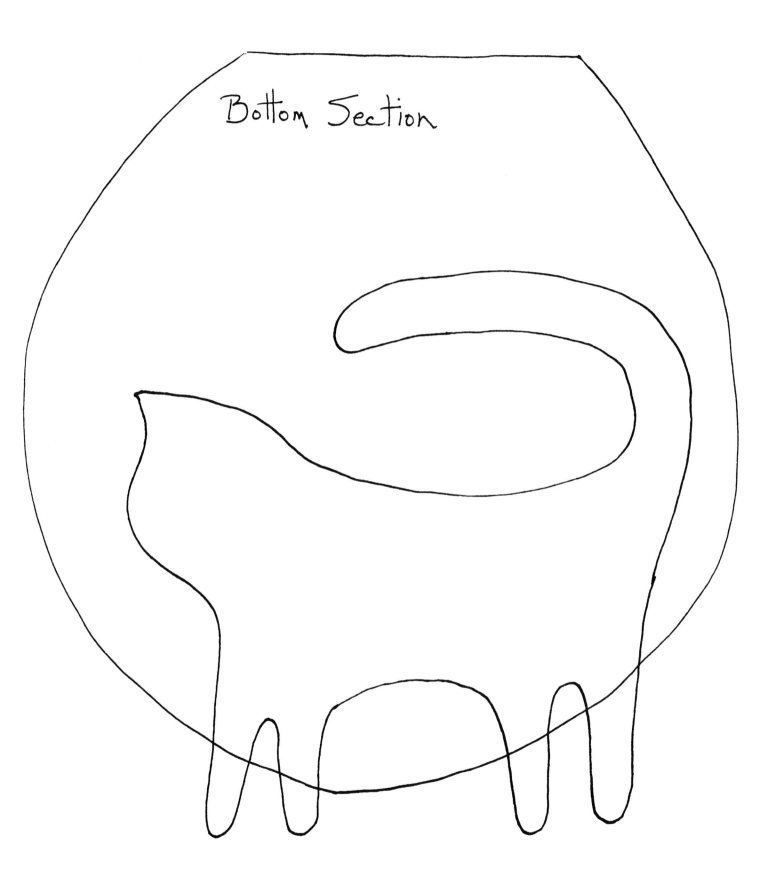

Bottom Section

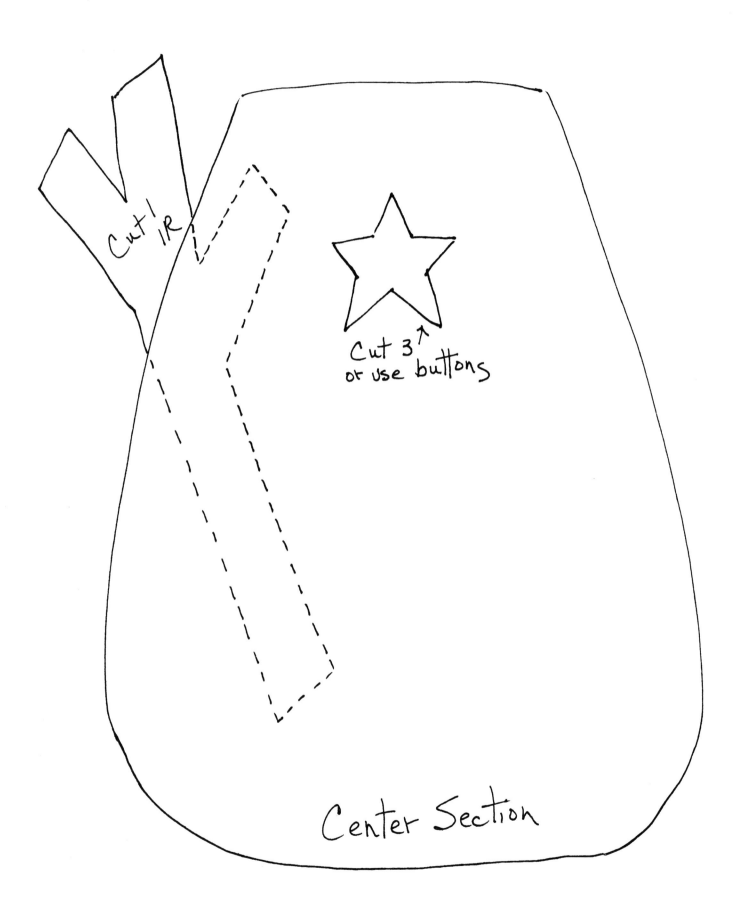

Cut 1R

Cut 3
or use buttons

Center Section

Spiced Pumpkin
Size 48" x 48"

Fabric Requirements:

- Center background: 5/8 yd
- Inner sawteeth: Fat quarter of light and dark fabrics
- Large corners on outer border and stars: 1/4 yard
- Setting triangles: 5/8 yard
- Outer pumpkin: Fat quarter
- Middle pumpkin: Fat quarter
- Center pumpkin: Fat quarter
- Vines: Fat quarter
- Leaves: Fat eighth and scraps
- Pumpkin blossoms: Fat eighth
- Birds: 1/4 yard
- Bird wings: Fat eighth
- Stop border: 1/4 yard
- Outer border sawteeth: 1/2 yard of dark and 1/4 yard of 2 lights
- Binding: 2/3 yard

Instructions:

(These measurements include seam allowance)
Cut 1 background block 20 1/2" x 20 1/2".

- Refer to the General Instructions and make freezer paper appliqué templates. Match the lines marked X and Y when making the large pumpkin template.
- Place the shapes on the background.
- Pin, glue stick or baste the shapes into place on the background. Appliqué in place.
- Make 40 - 2" finished half-square triangles. Use triangle paper or cut 20 - 2 7/8" squares of light and dark fabrics. Cut in half once on the diagonal and sew one light to one dark. Open and press toward the darkest fabric. Sew 10 half-square triangles together to make a strip. Make four strips. Sew one strip to one side of the square and one strip to the opposite side of the square. Cut four 2 1/2" orange squares. Sew a square to each end of the two remaining half-square triangle strips. Sew one strip to the top of the center square and one to the bottom.

- Cut 2 -17 7/8" squares. Cut each square once on the diagonal to make four setting triangles. Use freezer paper appliqué to appliqué the vines, leaves, blossoms, stars and birds to the setting triangles. Stitch the bird's eye and the veins on the leaves using 1 strand of linen floss or 2 strands of cotton. Refer to the General Instructions to learn how to make freezer paper templates. Sew the setting triangles to the center square with the sawteeth border.

Borders:

- Cut 2 - 36 1/2" x 1 1/2" stop borders and sew to sides.
- Make 24 - 6" finished half-square triangles. Cut 12 - 6 7/8" squares of light and dark fabrics. Cut in half once on the diagonal and sew one light to one dark. Open and press toward the darkest fabric.
- Sew half-square triangles into 4 rows of 6 squares each.
- Refer to the photo and sew two rows to opposite sides of the background square.
- Cut 4 - 6 1/2" squares. Sew a square to each end of the remaining two rows of half-square triangles.
- Sew the rows of half-square triangles to the remaining sides of the center.

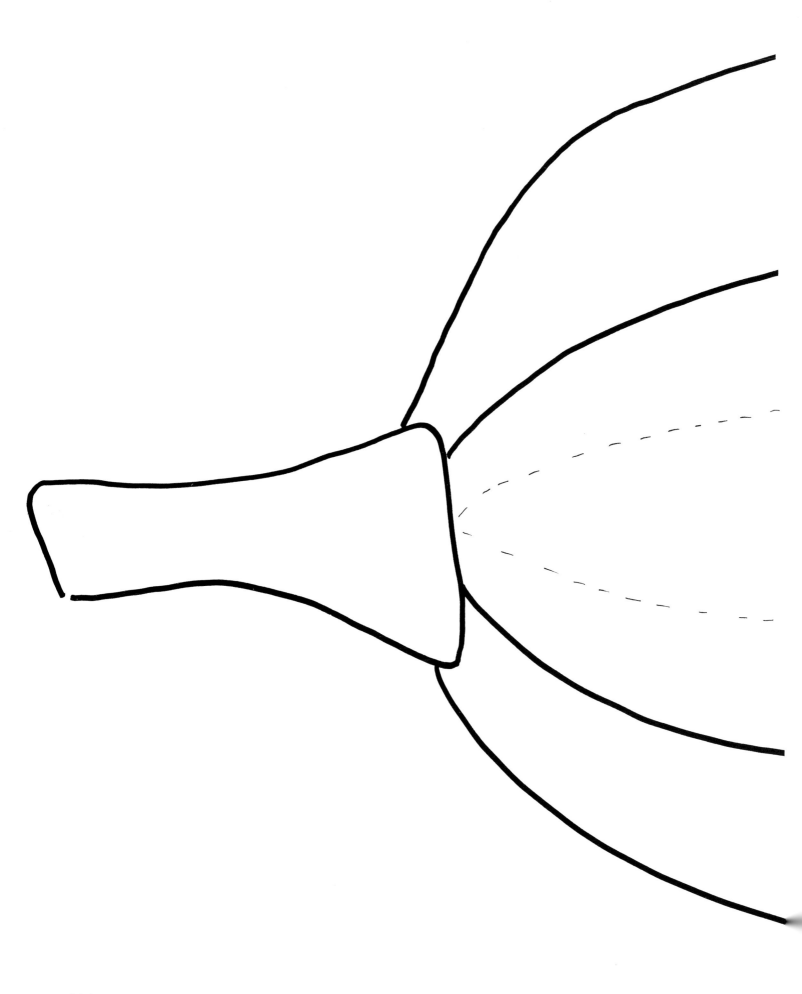

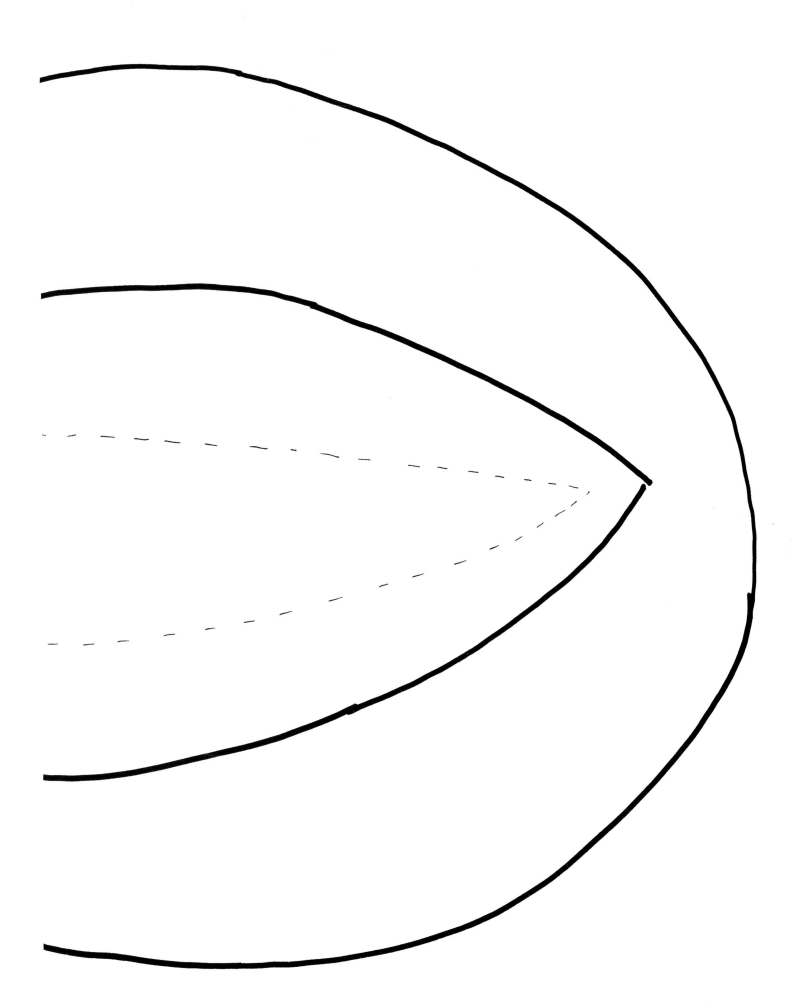

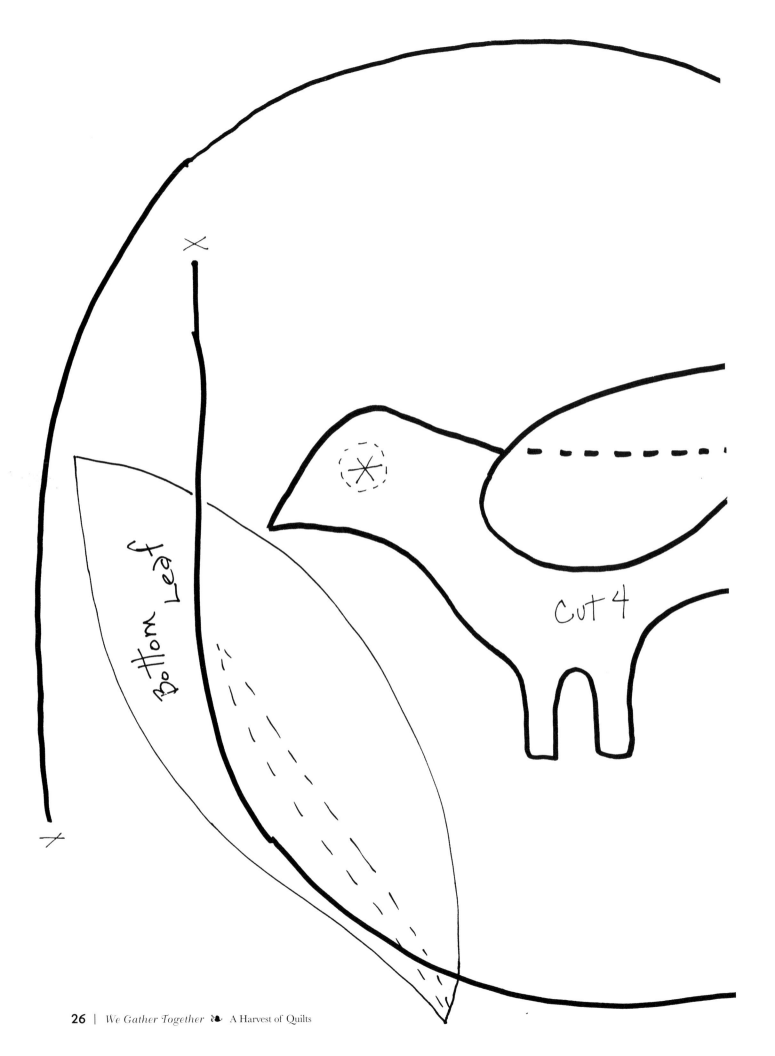

Bottom Leaf

Cut 4

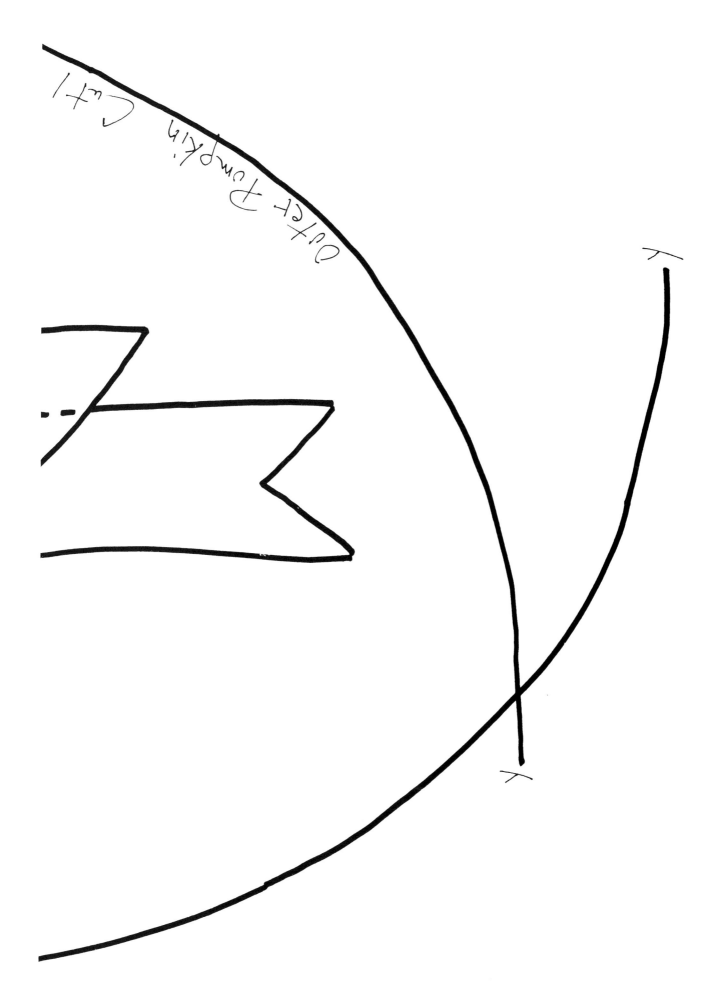

Outer Pumpkin Cut 1

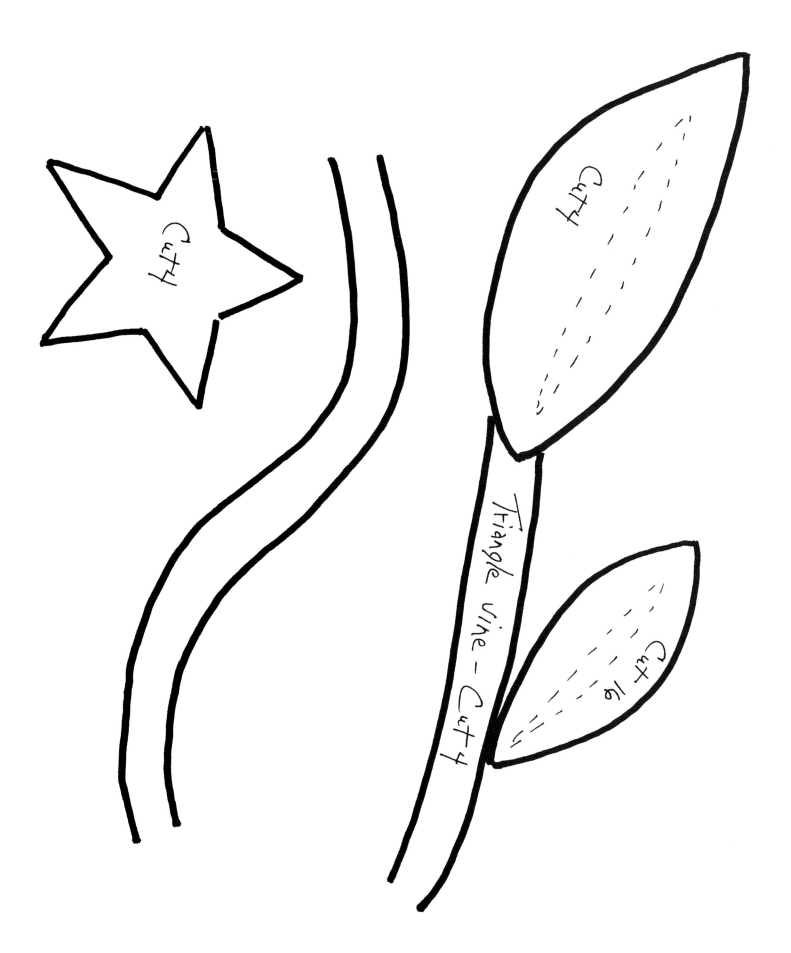

Cut 4

Cut 4

Cut 4

Triangle Vine — Cut 4

Cut 16

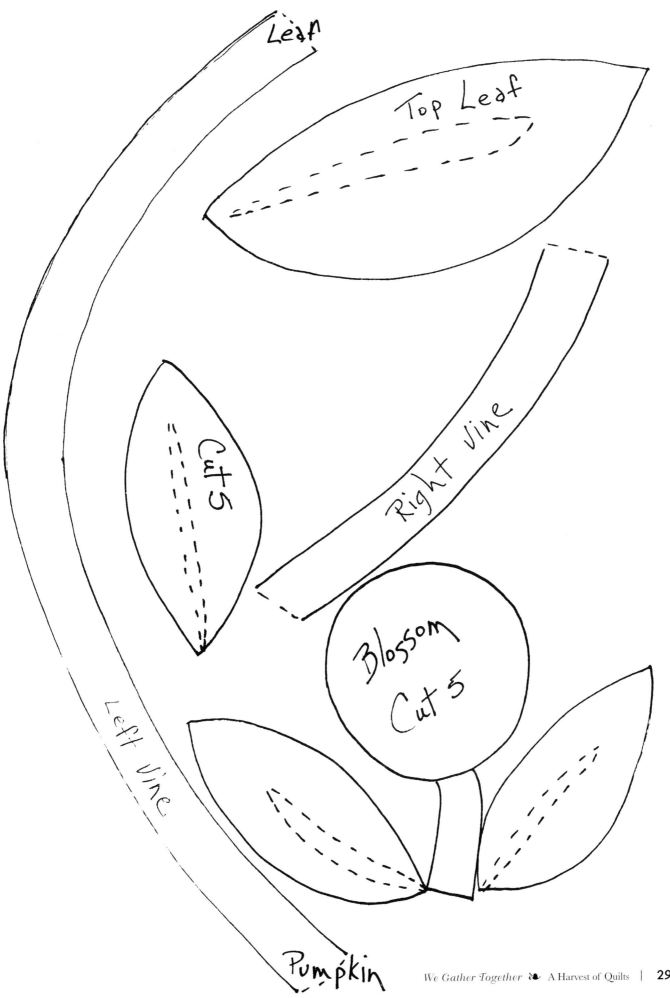

Leaf

Top Leaf

Right Vine

Cut 5

Blossom
Cut 5

Left Vine

Pumpkin

Moon Garden Pumpkins
Size: 36" x 30"

Fabric Requirements:

- Background: Total of 3/4 yard for background (or 2 fat quarters and a fat eighth if you piece it)

- Moon: 1/3 yard

- House front, house side, roof and door, windows, chimney, cat, scarecrow, pumpkins and stars: Scraps

- Inner border and saw teeth: 1/8 yard of 2 fabrics and 1/4 yd of another.

- 2" half-square triangles: Scraps

- 5 medium to darks and 5 lights for 3" half-square triangles: Scraps

- Outer borders: 1/4 yard

- Binding: 5/8 yard

Instructions:

(all measurements include seam allowances)

- From the background fabric, cut

  - 1 - 19 1/2" x 12 1/2" rectangle

  - 1 - 19 1/2" x 8 1/2" rectangle. Refer to the photo and sew the two pieces together.

  - 1 - 7 1/2" x 20 1/2" rectangle. Sew to the right side.

- Make freezer paper templates for all appliqué pieces. Refer to the General Instructions if necessary.

- Place the shapes on the background and pin, glue stick or baste the shapes into place on the background. Appliqué in place.

- Cut 2 - 20 1/2" x 2 1/2" borders and sew them to the sides.

- Make 4 - 2" finished half-square triangles. Cut 2 - 2 7/8" squares from the light and medium

fabrics. Cut in half once on the diagonal and sew one light to one medium to make 3 half-square triangles. Save the remaining light triangle and put away the remaining medium triangle for another project. Press toward the darkest fabric.

- Cut 1 - 2 7/8" square of dark fabric. Cut in half diagonally and sew the remaining light triangle to the dark to make the fourth half-square triangle.

- Cut 2 - 26 1/2" x 2 1/2" borders for the top and bottom of the quilt. Refer to the photo and sew a half-square triangle to each end of top and bottom border. Sew in place.

- Make 17 - 3" finished half-square triangles using the above directions but cutting 9 - 3 7/8" squares of light and 9 squares of medium to dark fabrics.

- Cut 1 - 21 1/2" x 3 1/2" top border. Refer to the photo and sew to 3 half-square triangles. Sew to the top of the quilt. (If you have trouble getting your triangle squares going in the right direction, it helps to lay each section out to make sure it looks like the photo - then sew it together.)

- Cut 1 - 24 1/2" x 3 1/2" bottom border. Refer to the photo and sew to 2 half-square triangles. Sew to the bottom of the quilt.

- Cut 1 - 15 1/2" x 3 1/2" left border. Refer to the photo and sew to 5 half-square triangles. Sew to the left side of the quilt.

- Cut 1 - 9 1/2" x 3 1/2" right border. Refer to the photo and sew to 7 half-square triangles. Sew to the right side of the quilt.

- Quilt as desired.

Cut 3

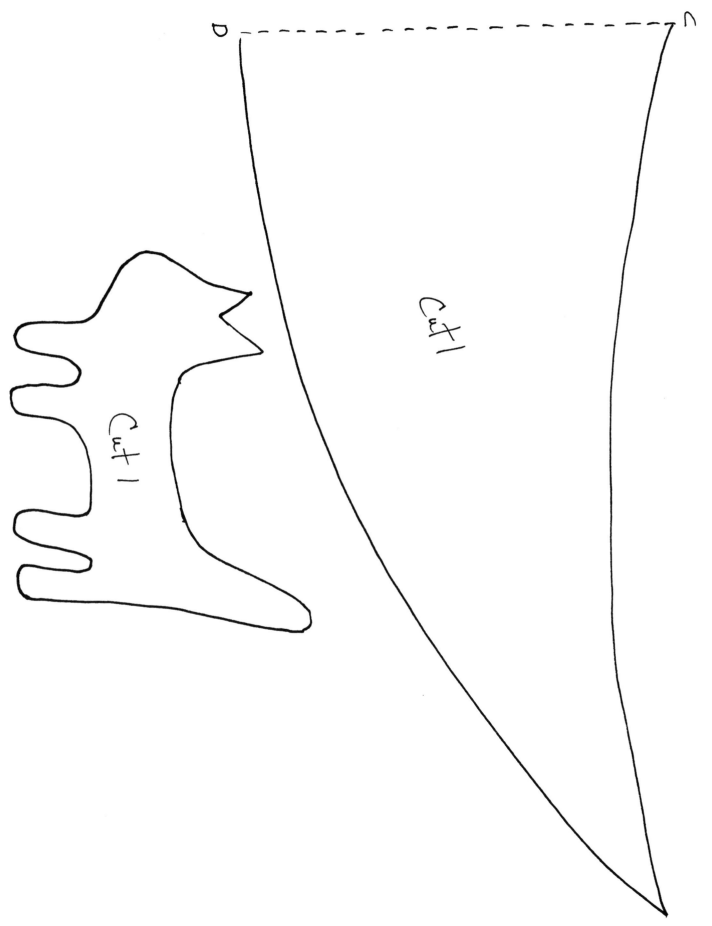

Cut 1

Cut 1

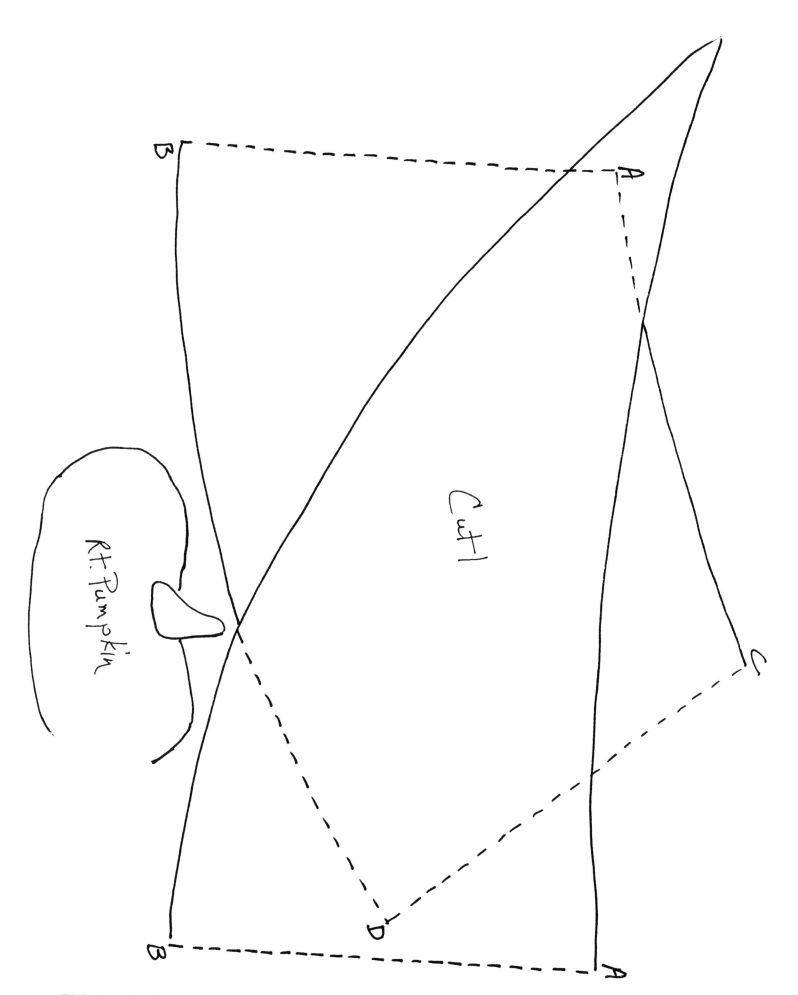

Rt. Pumpkin

Cut

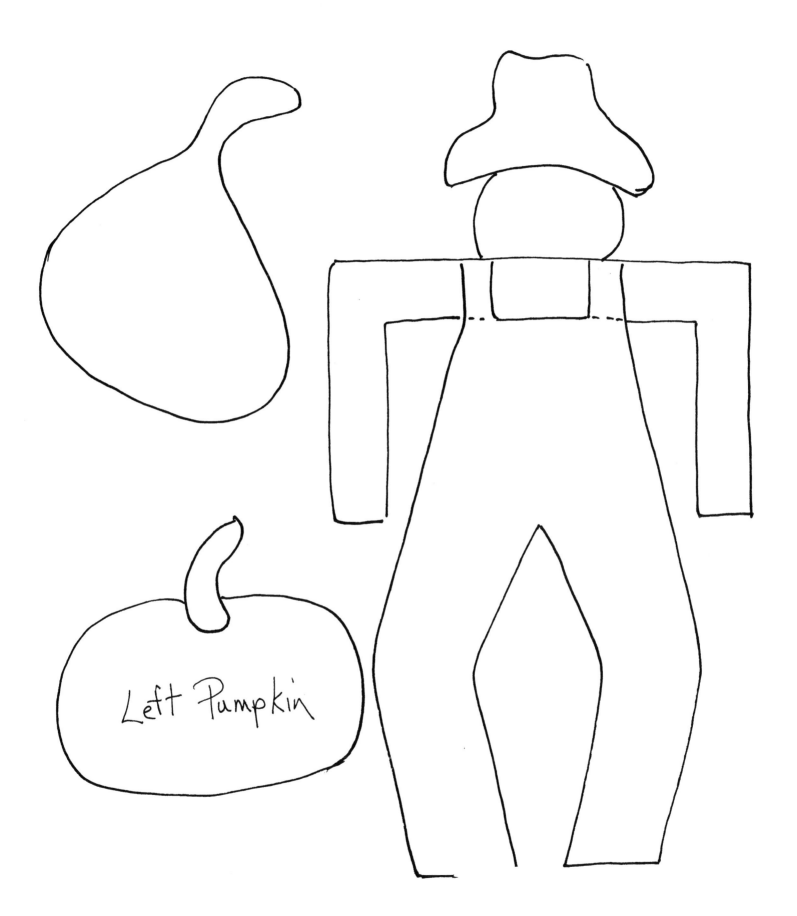

Left Pumpkin

We Gather Together

Size: 45" x 46"

Fabric Requirements

- Large background: 3/4 yard

- Blackbird background and right side strip: 1/3 yard

- Half-square triangles: 1/2 yard of light and a fat eighth each of 7 varied prints and homespuns

- Star background & star: Fat quarter of 2 fabrics

- Basket backgrounds and baskets: Fat quarter for backgrounds (includes strip for bottom block), fat eighth for each basket

- House: Fat quarter

- Roof & chimneys: Fat quarter

- Windows & door: Scraps

- Blackbirds: 1/4 yard with scraps for wings

- Flag: Scraps of red stripe print for flag, blue for field, cream for star and a 1 1/2" x 20 1/4" brown strip for pole

- Turkey: 1/3 yard for turkey and wing, scraps for feet and wattle and scraps for markings on tail and wing

- Pumpkins: Fat eighth for large pumpkin, fat eighth for smaller pumpkin with scraps for stems

- Leaves: Scraps of 6 varied prints and homespuns

- Right and bottom borders: 1/2 yard of large print

- Left and top borders: 1/3 yard of smaller print or homespun

- Binding: 2/3 yard

Instructions:

Cut the background blocks referring to the diagram. The diagram gives finished measurements for all elements so be sure and add 1/2" to everything.

- Make freezer paper templates for all appliqué pieces. Cut the background blocks referring to the diagram. The diagram gives finished measurements for all elements so be sure and add 1/2" to everything.

- Place the shapes on the background.

- Pin, glue stick or baste the shapes into place on the background.

- Appliqué the house, birds, flag and baskets to backgrounds.

- Cut and piece the star block using freezer paper templates.

- Draw your pattern block on the matte side of the freezer paper. Label all sections of your block. Cut them apart and iron the shiny side of the freezer paper to the right side of the fabric, (iron to the wrong side if you need the pattern reversed), allowing enough room to add your 1/4" seam allowance. Use a ruler to add the 1/4" seam allowance to each template. Then either mark the cutting line with a pencil and use scissors or if you are using a ruler to measure the 1/4" seam allowance, cut at the edge of the ruler with a rotary cutter.

- Sew together the main body of the wall hanging (minus the Broken Dish blocks and borders).

- Make 6 - 3" finished half-square triangles of the light fabric and five medium to dark fabrics.

Either use triangle paper or cut 3 - 3 7/8" squares of each fabric and 15 squares of light. Cut in half once on the diagonal and sew one light to one dark to make 6 half-square triangles of each color combination. Open and press toward the darkest fabric.

᠔ Make 8 - 3" finished half-square triangles using the light fabric and 2 dark to medium fabrics. Cut 2 - 3 7/8" squares of each medium to dark fabric and 4 squares of light print. Cut in half once on the diagonal and sew one light to one dark to make 6 half-square triangles of each color combination. Open and press toward the darkest fabric.

᠔ Refer to the photo for color placement and make 11 1/2 Broken Dish blocks.

᠔ Sew to the top and left side of the appliqué blocks. (It helps to lay each section out to make sure it looks like the photo before sewing it together.)

Borders:

᠔ Cut a 41 1/2" x 4 1/2" top border. Mark at 2 1/2" from the left side. Sew the border to the top until you are within 2 1/4" of the left edge of the border. Leave this hanging loose.

᠔ Cut a 40 1/2" x 4 1/2" right border and sew it to the right side.

᠔ Sew the appliquéd bottom border to the quilt.

᠔ Cut a 42 1/2" x 2 1/2" left border. Sew it to the left side.

᠔ Now go back to the top border (left hanging loose) and finish your seam.

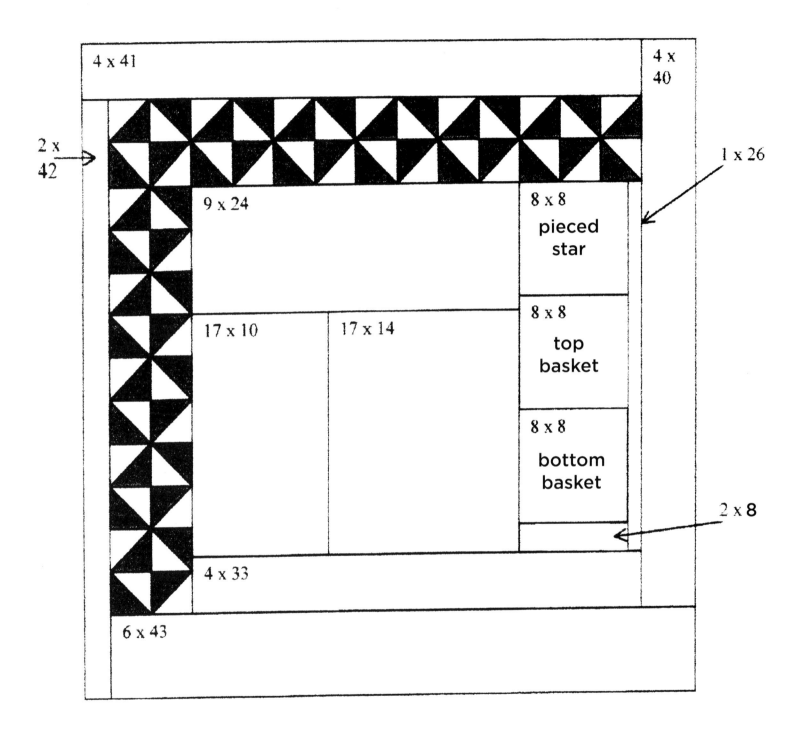

4 x 41

4 x 40

2 x 42

1 x 26

9 x 24

8 x 8
pieced
star

8 x 8
top
basket

17 x 10

17 x 14

8 x 8
bottom
basket

2 x 8

4 x 33

6 x 43

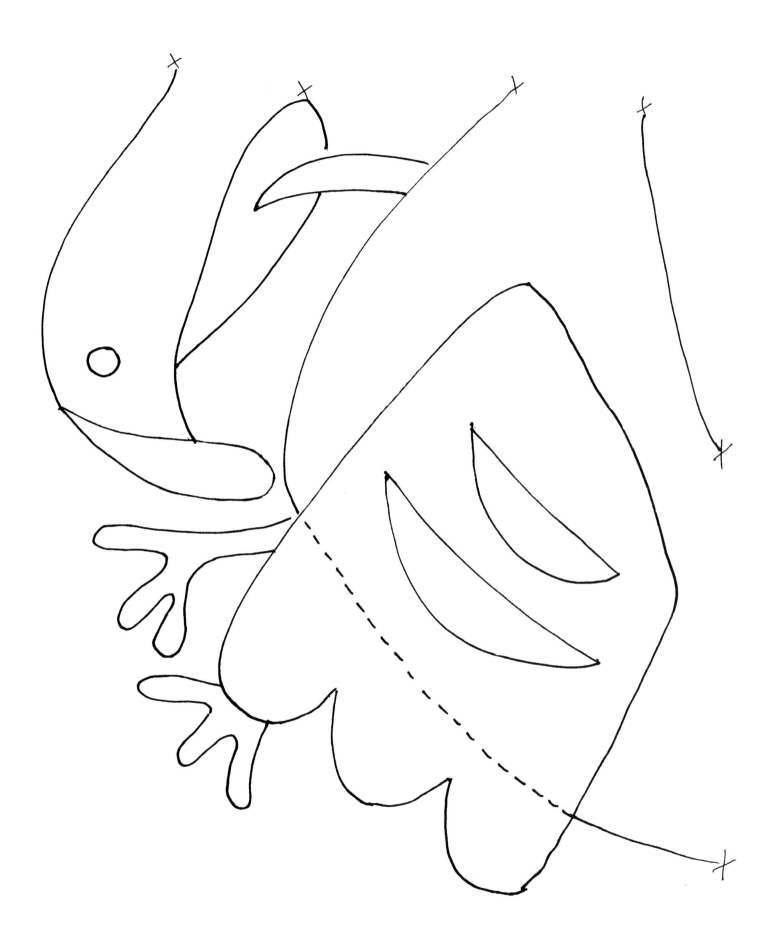

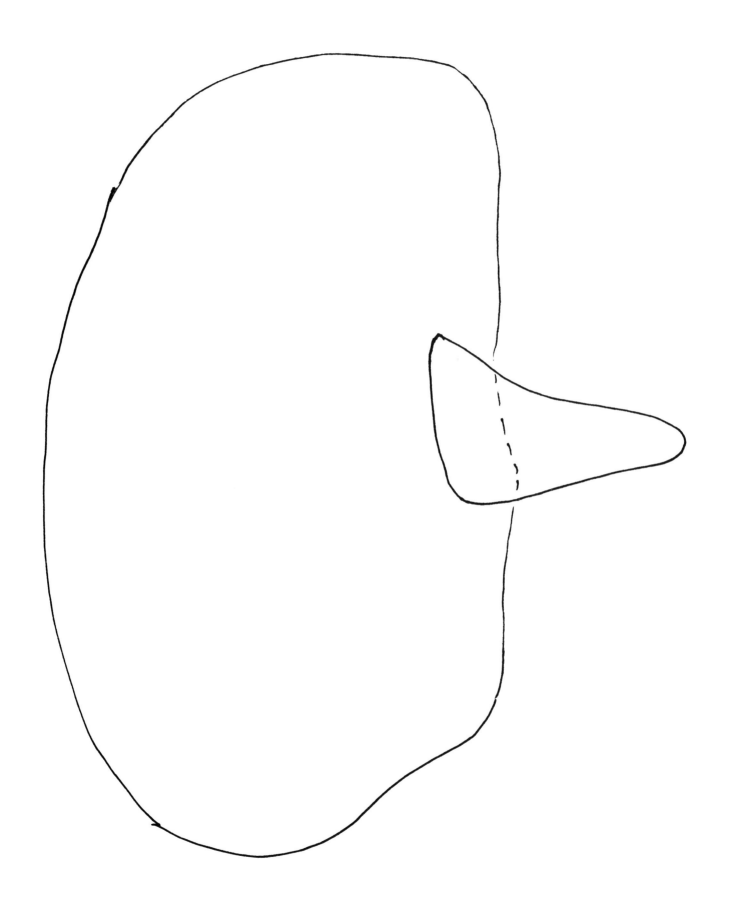

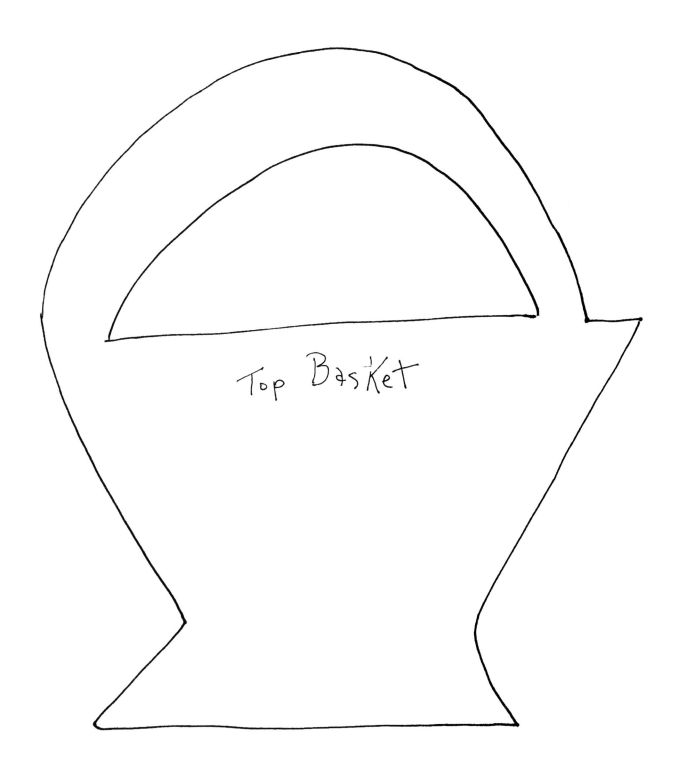

Top Basket

Bottom Basket

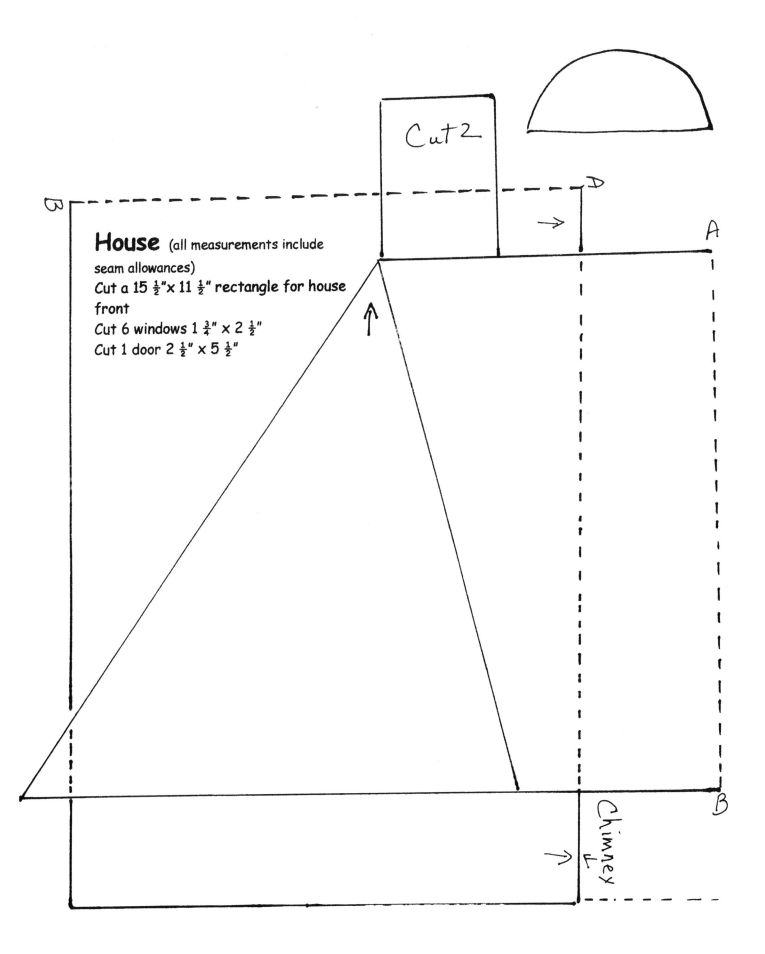

House (all measurements include seam allowances)
Cut a 15 ½" x 11 ½" rectangle for house front
Cut 6 windows 1 ¾" x 2 ½"
Cut 1 door 2 ½" x 5 ½"

Cut 2

B

A

A

B

Chimney

Cut 5

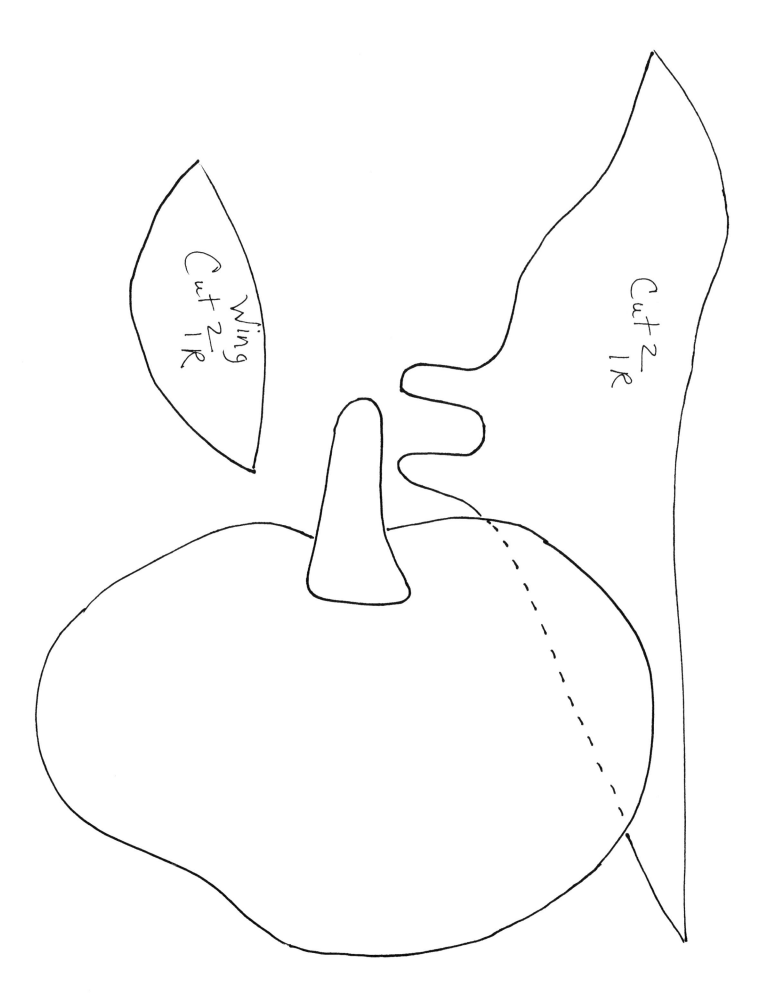

Wing
Cut 2
1 R

Cut 2
1 R

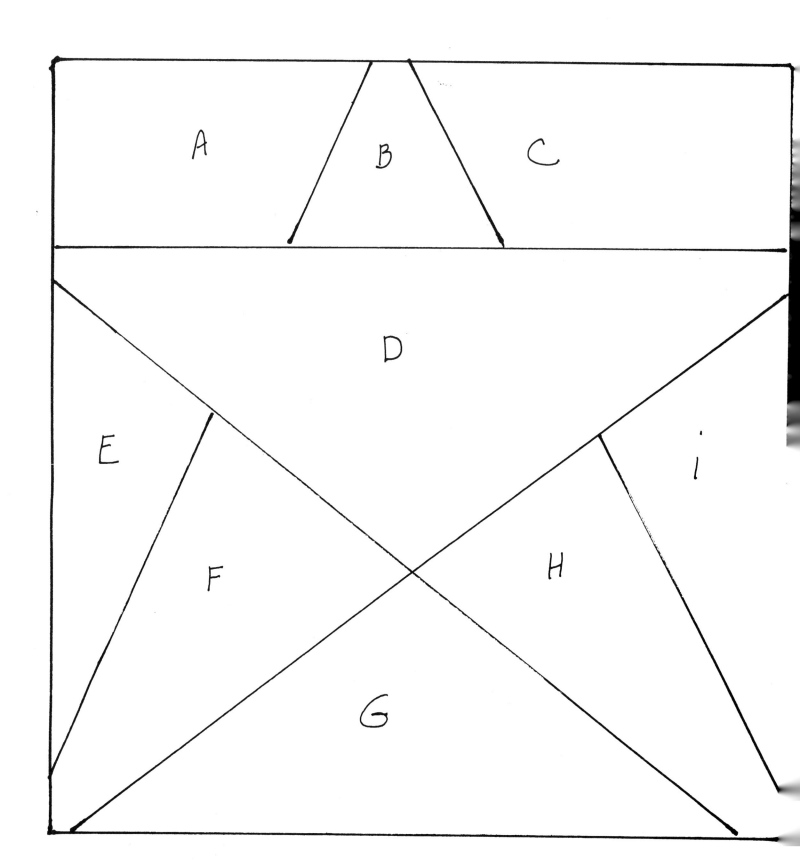

Shoo Crow

Size: 33" x 22"

Fabric Requirements:

- Background of pumpkins block: 1 fat quarter
- Background of scarecrow: 1 fat eighth
- Background of cat: 1 fat eighth
- Pumpkins: 3 different fat eighths
- Pumpkin stems, scarecrow, shirt, hat, cat, bird, stars and flying geese: Scraps
- Scarecrow overalls: 1 fat eighth
- Borders: 1/4 yard each of light, medium and dark
- Flying Geese in border: Scraps
- Binding: 5/8 yard
- Star button for bird's eye
- Cotton or linen floss

Instructions:

(All measurements include seam allowances.)

- Cut a 19 1/2" x 16 1/2" background block for the pumpkins. Cut an 8 1/2" x 5 1/2" background block for the cat. Using the freezer paper template directions in General Instructions, cut and piece the scarecrow block. Refer to the photo and sew the scarecrow block and the background blocks for the pumpkins and the cat together. Cut out and appliqué the pumpkins, stems and bird to the backgrounds.
- Using 2 strands of cotton floss or one strand of linen floss, embroider the wing on the bird and the lines on the pumpkins. Sew a star button eye on the bird after quilting.
- Make 9 - 2" x 4" (finished size) flying geese out of 18 - 2" finished half-square triangles. Make 18 - 2" finished half-square triangles.

Use triangle paper or cut 9 - 2 7/8" squares of light and dark fabrics. Cut the squares in half diagonally and sew one light to one dark. Open and press toward the darkest fabric. Sew two half-square triangles together to make each flying goose.

Borders:

- Bottom Border: Cut a 27 1/2" x 2 1/2" strip of light border fabric and sew to the bottom.
- Top Border: Cut a 10 1/2" x 4 1/2" strip of dark border fabric and a 5 1/2" x 4 1/2" strip of light. Refer to the photo and sew a dark strip, a light strip and 6 flying geese together. Sew to the top.
- Left Border: Cut a 22 1/2" x 2 1/2" strip of dark fabric and sew to left side.
- Right Border: Cut a 5 1/2" x 4 1/2" strip of the medium fabric, a 9 1/2" x 4 1/2" strip of the light and a 2 1/2" x 4 1/2" strip of the light. Refer to the photo and sew the strips and 3 flying geese together. Sew to the right side.
- Appliqué the stars and moon to the wall hanging.
- Trace the bird wing and pumpkin lines on tulle with a permanent marker. Place the tulle over the quilt block and, using a quilt marker, retrace the lines. Embroider lines on the bird and pumpkins using two strands of cotton floss or 1 strand of linen floss.

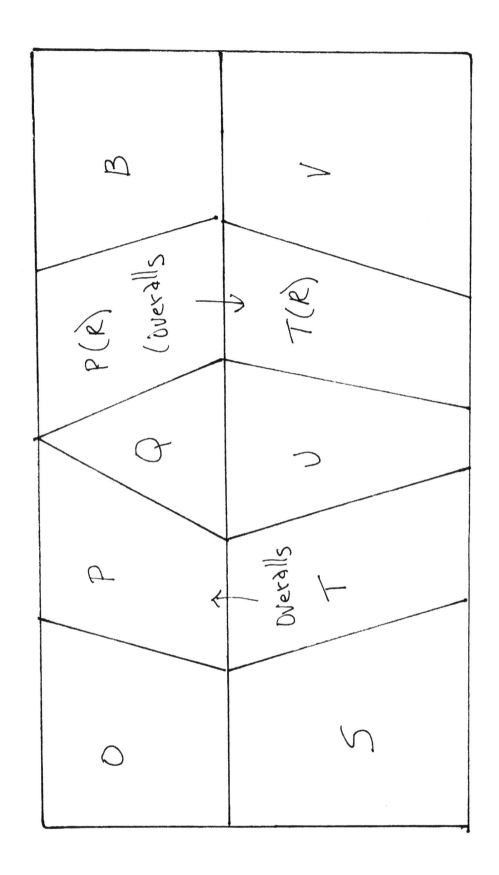

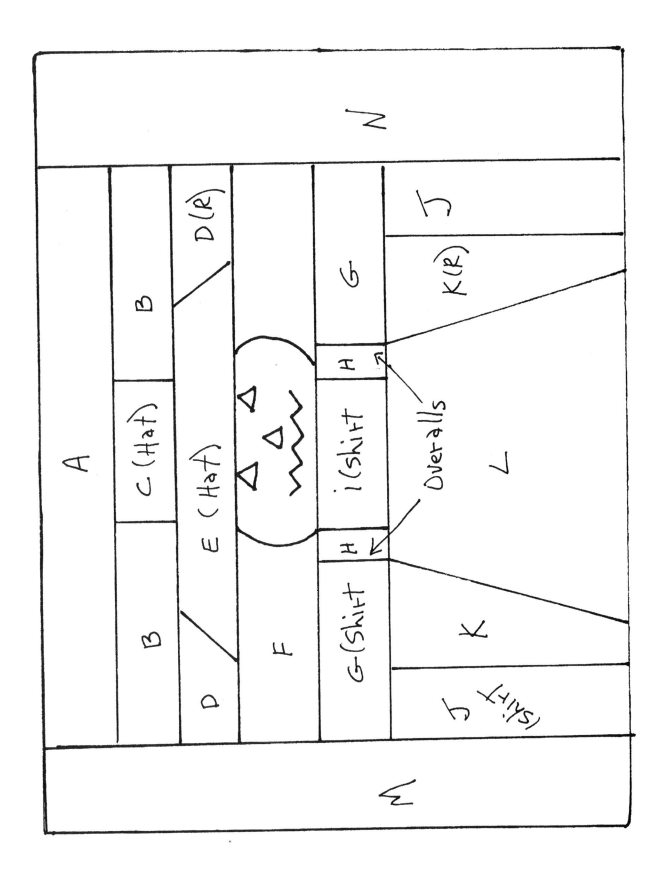

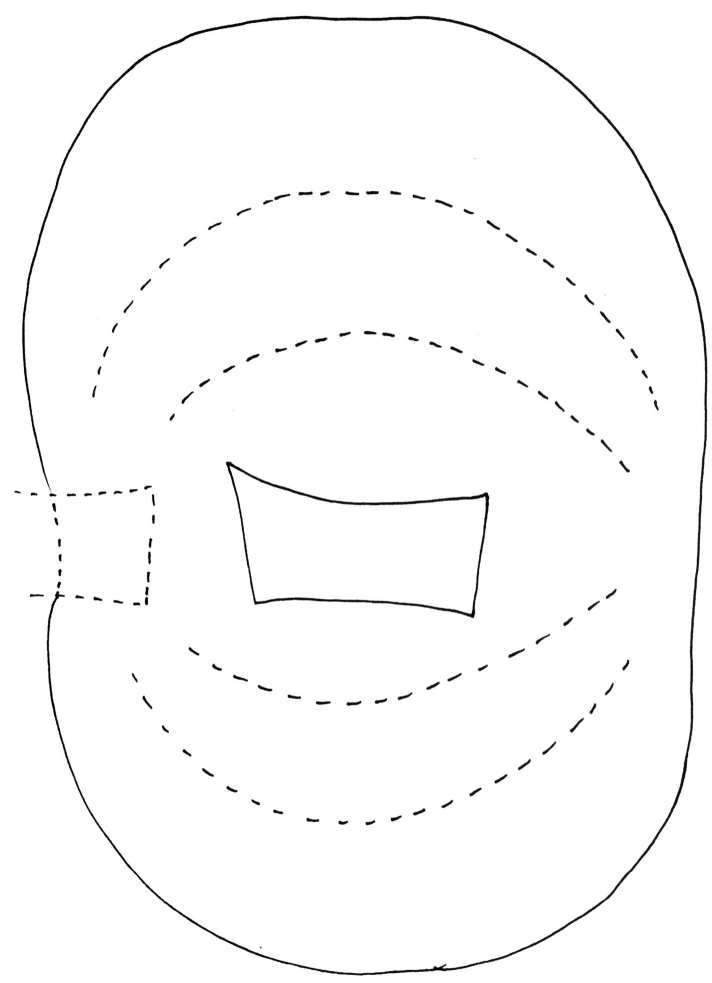

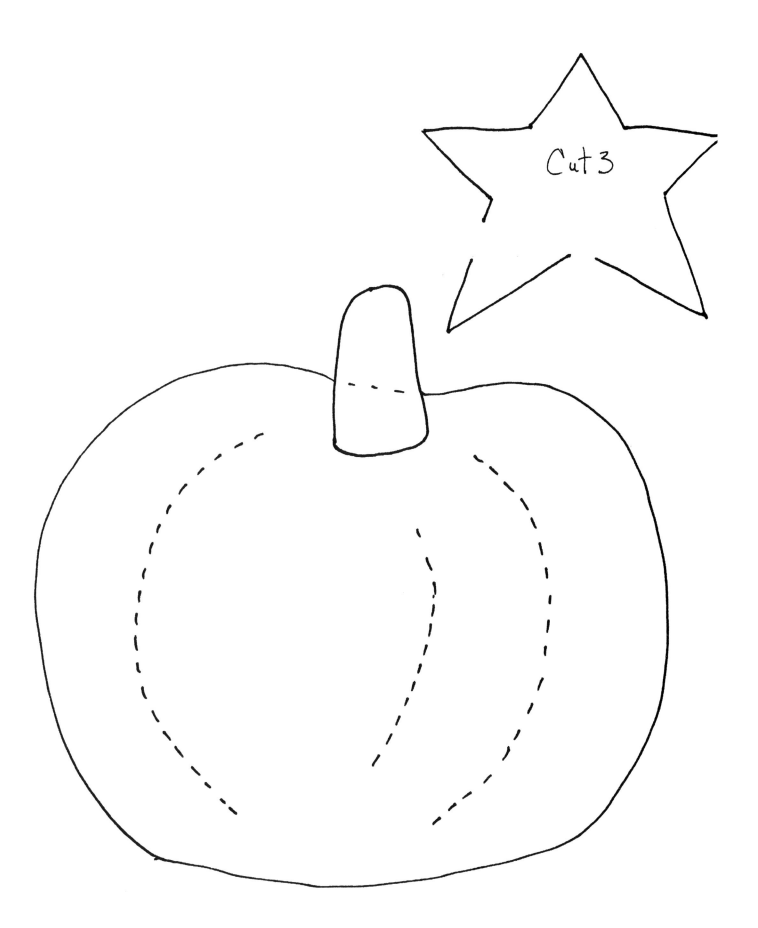

Cut 3

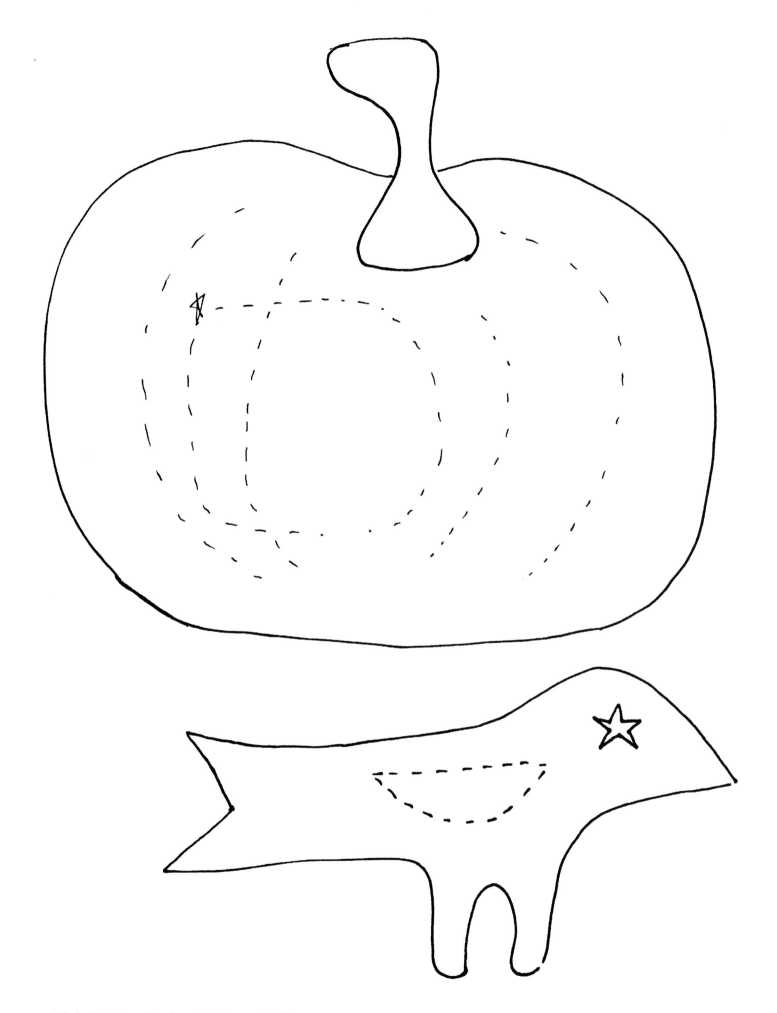

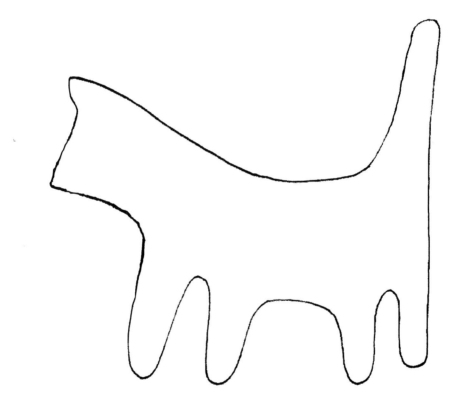

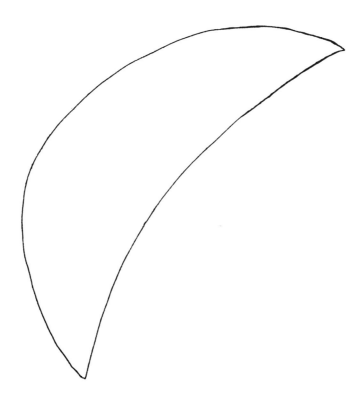

Pumpkin Wreath
Size: 35" x 35"

Designed by Jan Patek and Cherie Ralston
Appliquéd by Jan Patek
Quilted by Lori Kukuk

Fabric Requirements

- 3 background blocks: 1/2 yard

- Fourth background block: 1 fat quarter

- Stems, corner squares and pumpkin middle: 1/2 yard

- Dark leaves: 1/8 yard

- Lighter leaves: 1 fat eighth

- Blossoms: 1/8 yard

- Half-square triangles (includes berries): 1/2 yard of 2

- Outer pumpkin: Fat eighth and scraps for center

- Outer border: 1/2 yard

- Binding: 5/8 yard

Instructions:

(These measurements include seam allowances)

- Cut 4 - 12 1/2" x 12 1/2" background blocks.

- Refer to the photo and sew the four background blocks together. (Usually we appliqué each block before sewing the blocks together. In this pattern, we found it easier to achieve the circle or wreath effect if the blocks were sewn together first.)

- Using freezer paper applique, appliqué the pumpkin, stems, blossoms, berries and leaves in place. (Refer to the General Instructions to learn how to make freezer paper templates.)

- Place the shapes on the background, making sure that the stems are placed on each block in a manner suggesting a circle or wreath.

- Pin, glue stick or baste the shapes into place on the background.

- Make 48 - 2" finished half-square triangles.

- Use either triangle paper or cut 24 - 2 7/8" squares of light and dark fabrics. Cut in half once on the diagonal and sew one light to one dark. Open and press toward the darkest fabric.

- Sew the half-square triangles into two rows of 12 squares each and sew to the top and bottom. (If you have trouble getting your half-square triangles going in the right direction, it helps to lay each section out first to make sure it looks like the photo before sewing it together.)

- Sew the remaining half-square triangles into two rows of 12 squares each for the sides. Cut 4 - 2 1/2" squares and sew them to the end of the side row. Sew to the sides.

Borders:

- Cut two borders 28 1/2" x 4". Sew to the sides.

- Cut two borders 35 1/2" x 4". Sew to the top and bottom.

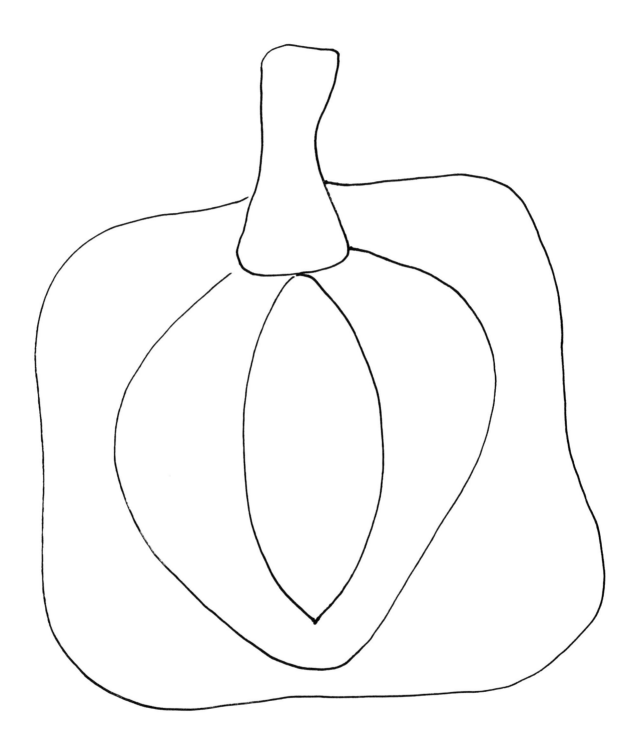

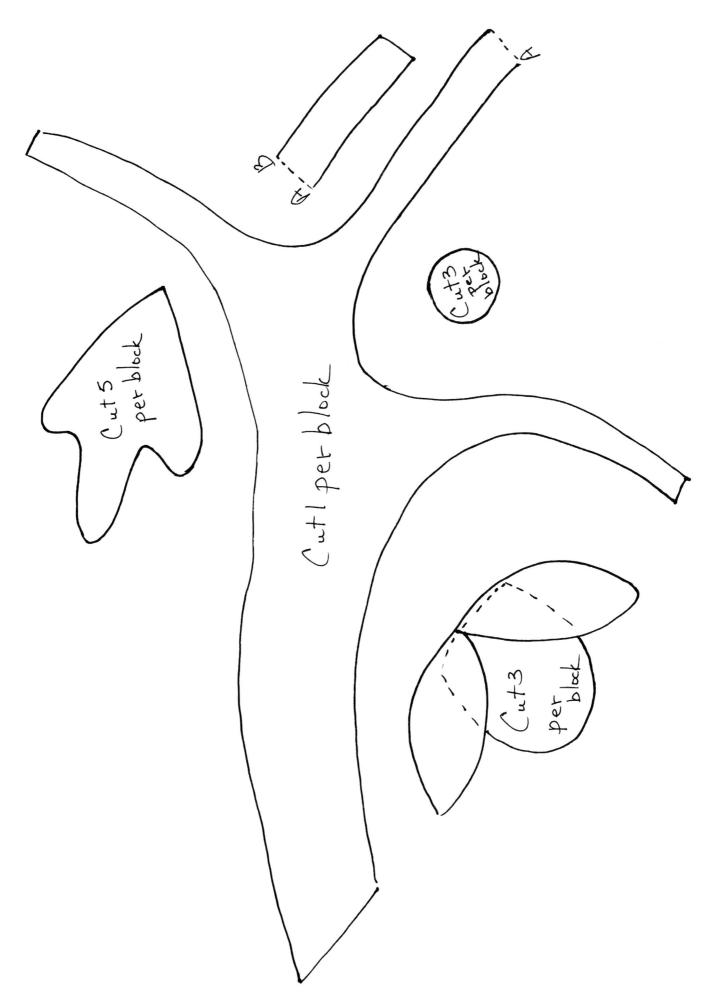

Cut 5 per block

Cut 1 per block

Cut 3 per block

Cut 3 per block

Pumpkin Patch

Size: 66" x 82"

Fabric Requirements:

- Nine-patch blocks: there are a total of 20 - 12" (finished) nine-patch blocks – 6 each of 3 color combinations and 2 each of 1 color combination as follows:

- 3 lights and 3 darks (we used tan and orange or rust) to make 6 blocks of each color combination: 1/2 yard each

- 1 light and 1 dark, (we used a tan/green twill and brown plaid) to make 2 blocks of this combination: 1 fat quarter each

- Borders & sashing: 1 2/3 yards of one (we used blue jacquard) and 2/3 yard of another (we used blue homespun stripe)

- Pumpkins:

  - Pumpkin #1: Fat eighth for pumpkin, scraps for markings

  - Pumpkin #2: Fat eighth for pumpkin

  - Pumpkin #3: Fat eighth for outer pumpkin, fat eighth for middle and inner pumpkin pieces

  - Pumpkin #4: Fat quarter for pumpkin, fat eighth for markings

  - Pumpkin #5: Fat quarter for pumpkin, fat eighth for markings

  - Pumpkin #6: Fat quarter of 2 for outer and middle pumpkin pieces, fat eighth for center piece. All pumpkin stems are scraps from green and pumpkin fabrics

- Birds: Scraps of black prints and homespuns for birds

- Stars: Scraps of 5 fabrics for stars

- Vine & Leaves: 1/2 yard

- Blossoms: Fat eighth

- Leaves: Scraps of 3 greens

- Binding: 7/8 yard

Instructions:

(all measurements includes seam allowances)

- Nine-patches

  - There are a total of 20 - 12" (finished) nine-patch blocks – 6 each of 3 color combinations and 2 each of 1 color combination.

  - From each of the three color combinations, cut 2 - 3 1/2" x 44" strips and 1 - 6 1/2" x 44" strip from each dark (pumpkin, rust or brown). Cut 2 - 3 1/2" x 44" strips and 1 - 6 1/2" x 44" strip from each light. From the remaining color combinations, cut 2 - 3

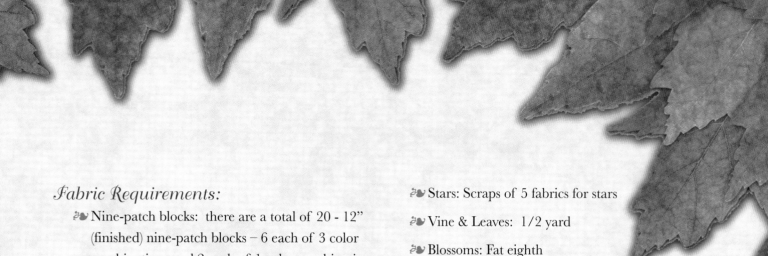

  1/2" x 22" and 1 - 6 1/2" x 22" strips. Sew the strips together referring to the diagram – one set of dark, light, dark and one set of light, dark, light.

  - Now cut 3 1/2" strips crosswise from the

dark/light/dark strips and 6 1/2" strips crosswise from the light/dark/light fabric.

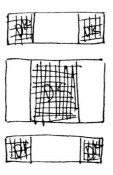

🍂 Piece 20 – 9-patch blocks.

Sashing strips:

(all measurements include seam allowances)

🍂 Cut 15 - 2 1/2" x 12 1/2" sashing strips

🍂 Refer to the diagram and sew the sashing strips and blocks into five rows of four.

🍂 Cut 2 - 54 1/2" x 2 1/2" sashing strips. Cut 2 - 54 1/2" x 3 1/2" sashing strips.

🍂 Refer to the diagram and sew the sashing strips and rows together.

Appliqué:

🍂 Use freezer paper appliqué to make your pumpkins, birds and stars. Refer to the General Instructions to learn how to make freezer paper templates.

🍂 Refer to the photo and pin, glue stick or baste the appliqué pieces to the background and appliqué in place. I like to sew the blocks and sashing into rows and do as much of the appliqué as possible before assembling the entire top.

Borders:

🍂 Cut 2 - 70 1/2" x 6 1/2" outer borders. Cut 1 - 15" square and make approximately 125 inches of 1/2" bias vine using bias instructions. Cut your bias strips 1" wide for 1/2" finished bias. Appliqué the vines, leaves and blossoms in place and sew to the sides.

🍂 Making the blossoms is a snap following this easy method.

🍂 Trace the circle the required number of times onto freezer paper. Cut the circles out. and iron the freezer paper to the wrong side of the fabric. Cut the fabric 1/4" larger than your pattern. (I keep my patterns and fabric circles in a Ziploc bag so I don't lose any.)   Make a knot in your thread and do a running stitch around the outer edge of fabric. Pull the thread until the fabric is snugly around the circle. Backstitch and cut your thread.   Appliqué the blossom to the background. Cut out the back and spray lightly with water if you used freezer paper. You can use tweezers to remove the paper.

🍂 Cut 2 - 66 1/2" x 6 1/2" outer borders. Appliqué the vine and leaves to the bottom border. Sew the top & bottom borders in place.

🍂 Refer to the photo and appliqué the remaining pumpkins and stars to top.

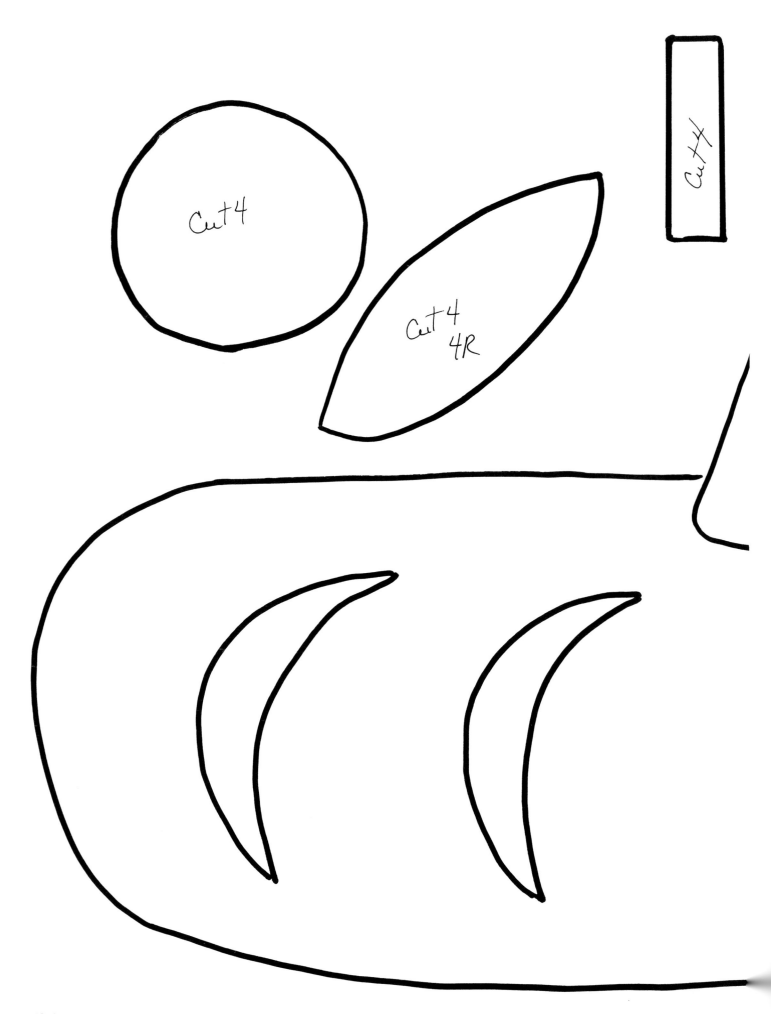

Cut 4

Cut 4
4R

Cut 4

Cut 4

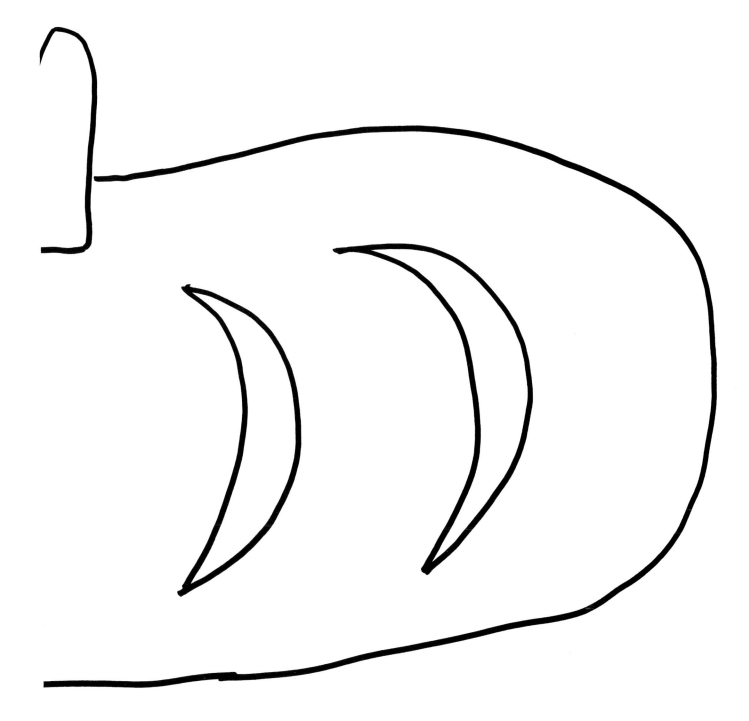

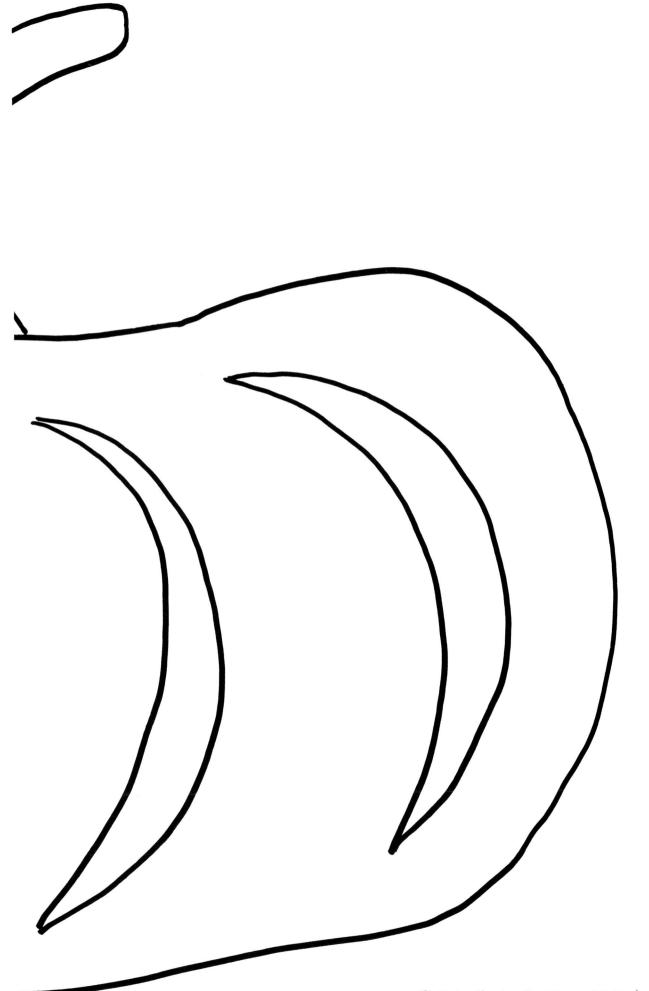

Cut 5

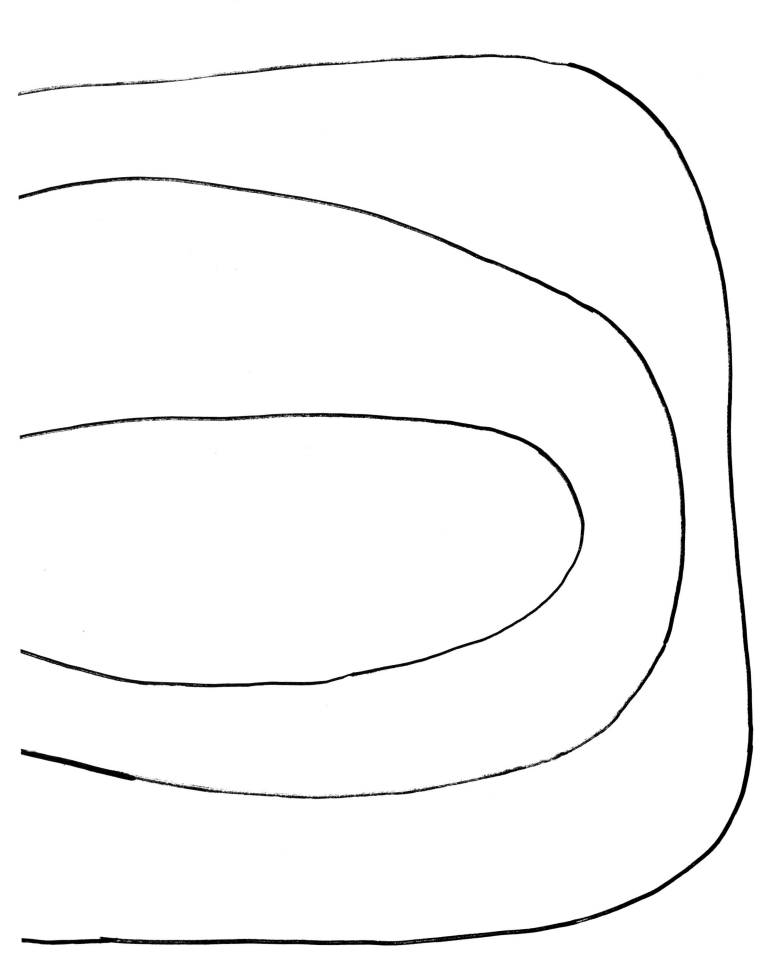

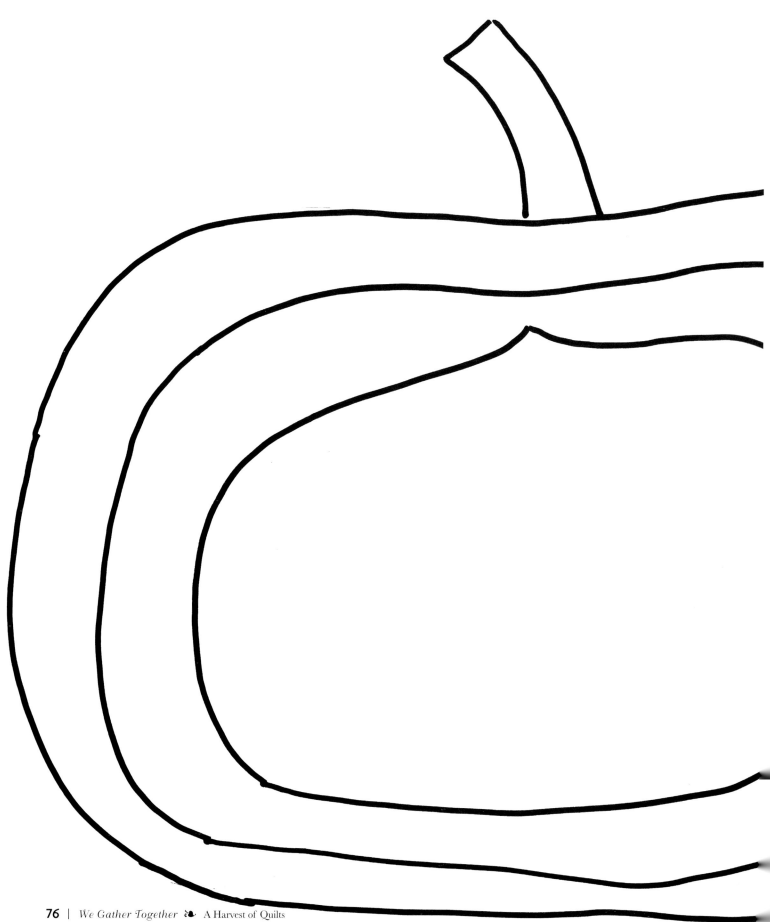

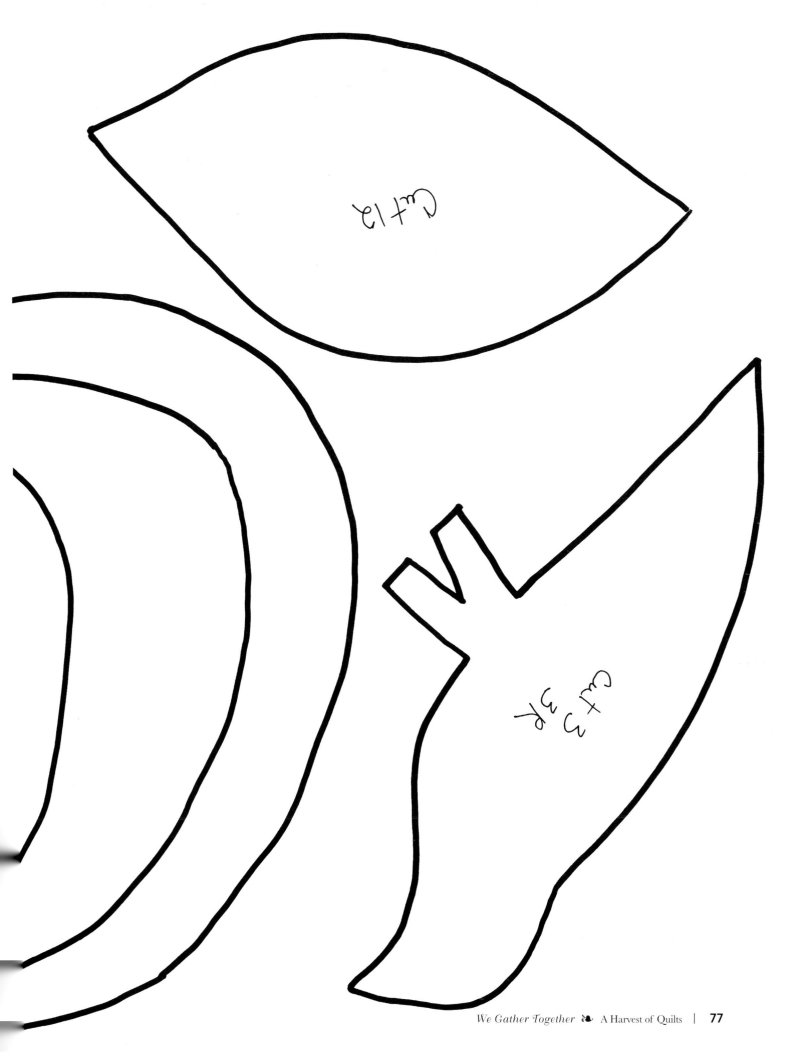

Cut 13

Cut 3 R

Happy Hollow

Size 76" x 74"

Fabric Requirements:

Refer to photo and diagram for placement

Backgrounds:

- Backgrounds of pumpkin #1 (top left), top border oak leaf/star block and the bottom left section of the house block: 1 yard

- Backgrounds of top left section of house block and Pumpkin #2 (pumpkin with bird): 1/2 yard

- Backgrounds of the top middle section of the house block and 2 border oak leaf/star blocks: 2/3 yard

- Background of right section of house block and vine block: 3/4 yard

- Background of large oak leaf/star block and pumpkin #3 (vine pumpkin): 1/2 yard

- Plaid background of 4" (finished) leaf squares: 1/2 yard

- Stop border and background of 4" (finished) leaf squares: 7/8 yard of print

- Background of 4" (finished) moon and star squares: 1/3 yard of print

- Border: 1 1/4 yard striped fabric

- Binding: 7/8 yard

Appliqué:

- 4" square leaves, vine, vine leaves, cockscomb leaves, sashing strips (2 - 2"x 8" finished) and all pumpkin stems: 3/4 yard

- Pumpkin #1 – Top left: Fat quarter for outer pumpkin, scraps for center

- Pumpkin #2 (Bird pumpkin): fat quarter for outer pumpkin, fat eighth for middle pumpkin

pieces, scraps for center of pumpkin, bird and wing

- Pumpkin #3 (Vine pumpkin): Fat quarter for outer pumpkin, scraps for markings

- Oak Leaf Blocks: 1/3 yard for oak leaves (also star on house) and fat eighth for stars

House Block:

- House front: Fat quarter

- House side: 5/8 yard

- Roof, chimneys and door: Fat eighth

- Windows: Scraps from star fabric in star block

- Star: Scraps of oak leaf fabric

- Moon: Scraps from background for Pumpkin #1 and lower left section of house background

- Cat: Fat eighth

- Cockscomb stem and 1 cockscomb leaf, 5 leaves on vine: 1/3 yard

- Flower: Fat eighth

- 4" Star and Moon Blocks: Fat quarter each for stars and moons

- 4" Leaf Blocks: 1/4 yard of gold for homespun leaves, see above for print leaves

Instructions:

(These measurements include seam allowance)

- Refer to the diagram and cut the backgrounds. All the measurements in the diagram are finished sizes so be sure to add the 1/2" seam allowance to all the background blocks.

- For the House Block, sew the background pieces

together before appliquéing.

- ❧ Cut the appliqué shapes from freezer paper. Refer to the General Instructions to learn how to make freezer paper templates.

- ❧ Pin, glue stick or baste the shapes into place on the backgrounds. Appliqué in place.

Big House pattern
(these measurements include seam allowance)

- ❧ Cut a 13" x 14 1/2" rectangle for the house front.

- ❧ Cut a 9 1/2" x 14 1/2" rectangle and a 9 1/2" x 6 1/2" rectangle for the side of the house. Draw a pattern on freezer paper using pattern A and C and cut rectangles the size given in the diagram. The measurements in the diagram do not include the seam allowance and don't need to since they are for the drawing for the pattern. After drawing the house side pattern according to the diagram, cut it out and proceed with regular freezer paper appliqué techniques.

- ❧ Cut 9 - 4 1/2" blocks and appliqué the stars in place.

- ❧ Cut 4 - 4 1/2" blocks and appliqué the small moons in place.

- ❧ Cut 27 - 4 1/2" blocks and appliqué the green small leaves in place.

- ❧ Cut 22 - 4 1/2" blocks and appliqué the gold small leaves in place.

- ❧ Cut 2 - 8 1/2" x 2 1/2" sashing strips of green.

We always piece our border strips so that is the yardage amount we have given. Cut the border strips and sew them end to end. Refer to the diagram and cut the following border pieces:

- 4 1/2" square - cut 1
- 4 1/2" x 8 1/2" - cut 9
- 4 1/2" x 12 1/2" - cut 5
- 4 1/2" x 16 1/2" - cut 6
- 4 1/2" x 20 1/2" - cut 1
- 4 1/2" x 24 1/2" - cut 1
- 4 1/2" x 32 1/2" - cut 1

Assembly:

- ❧ Refer to the photo and diagram and sew the inner appliqué blocks (house block, pumpkin blocks, vine and large oak leaf block) together with the moon, star, 4" leaf blocks and border strips. Cut 2 - 56 1/2" x 2 1/2" stop borders and sew to the top and bottom of the quilt. Cut 2 - 58 1/2" x 2 1/2" stop borders and sew to the sides of the quilt.

- ❧ Refer to the diagram and photo and piece the remaining leaf, star, moon, oak leaf and star blocks, sashing strips and border strips. When complete, stitch the side borders to the quilt, then add the top and bottom borders.

- ❧ Quilt as desired.

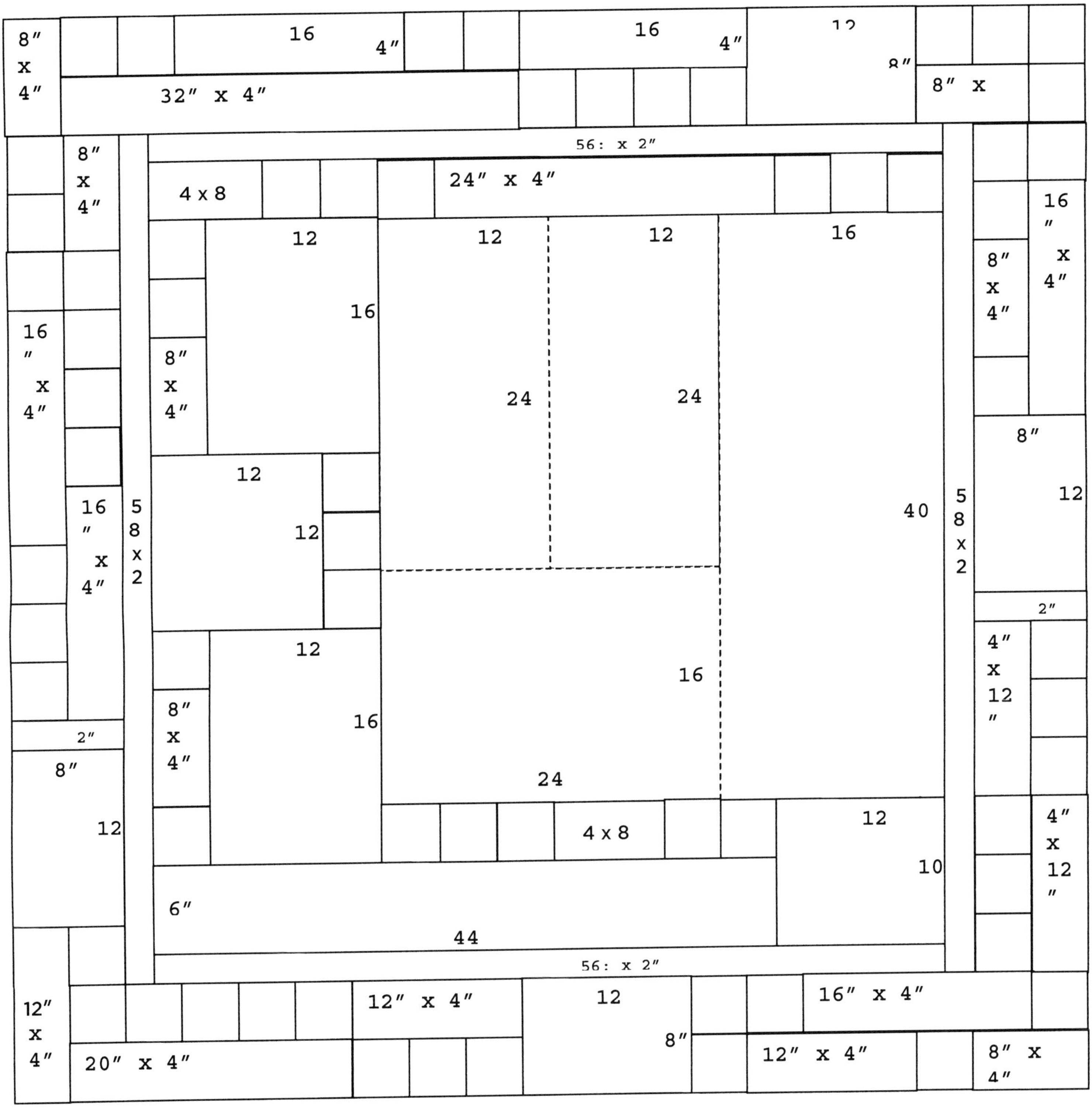
8″ x 4″
16
4″
16
4″
12
8″
32″ x 4″
8″ x
56: x 2″
8″ x 4″
4 x 8
24″ x 4″
16 ″ x 4″
12
16
12
12
16
16 ″ x 4″
8″ x 4″
8″ x 4″
24
24
8″
12
12
16 ″ x 4″
5 8 x 2
12
40
5 8 x 2
2″
4″ x 12 ″
12
16
8″ x 4″
16
2″
8″
12
24
4″ x 12 ″
4 x 8
12
10
6″
44
56: x 2″
12″ x 4″
12″ x 4″
12
16″ x 4″
8″
20″ x 4″
12″ x 4″
8″ x 4″

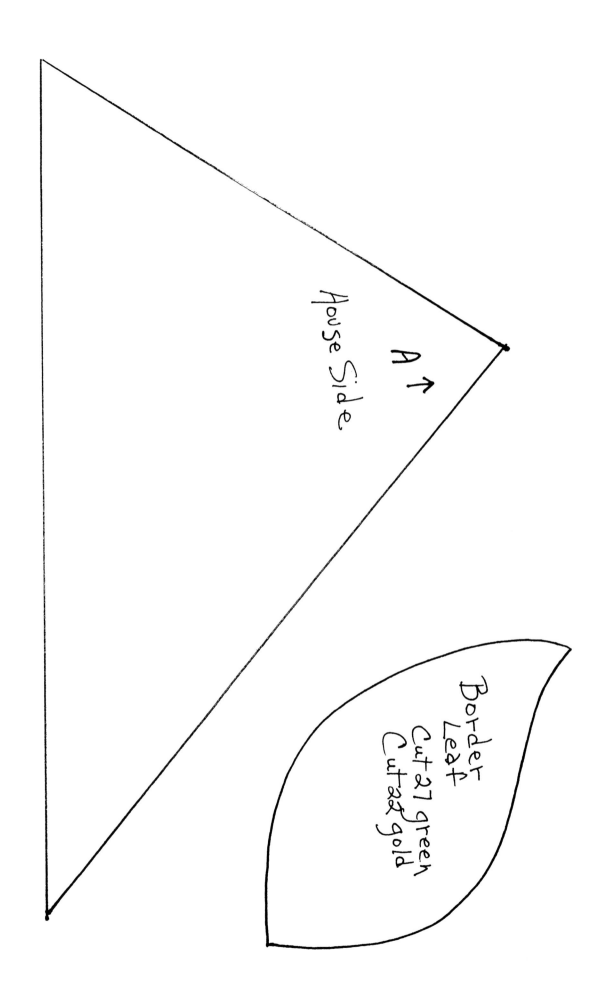

House Side

A ↑

Border
Leaf
Cut 27 green
Cut 27 gold

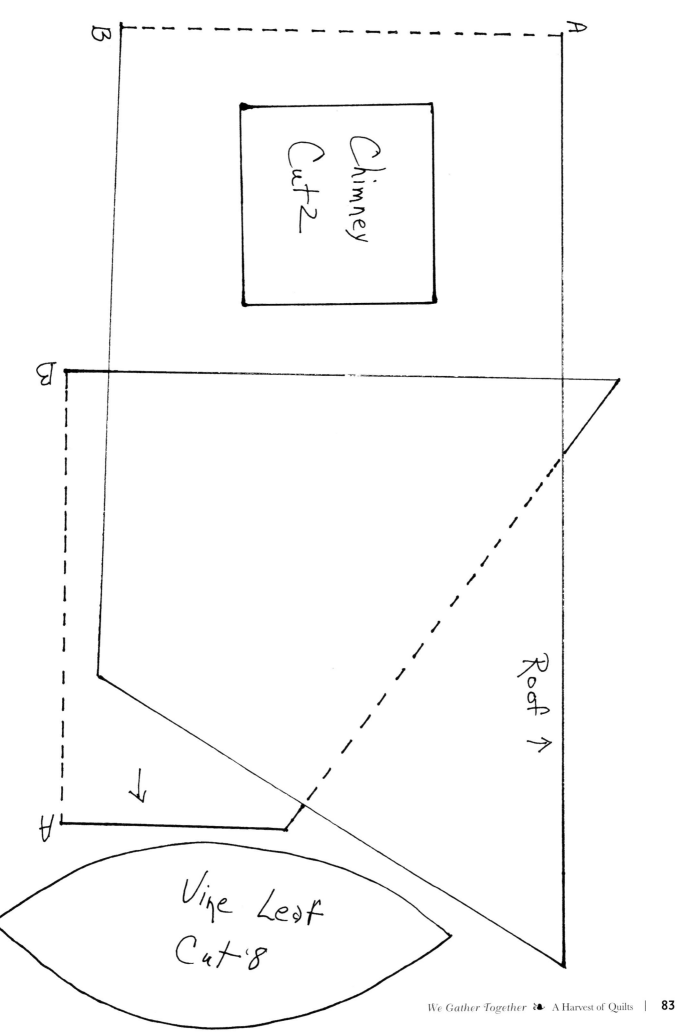

Chimney
Cut 2

Roof →

Vine Leaf
Cut 8

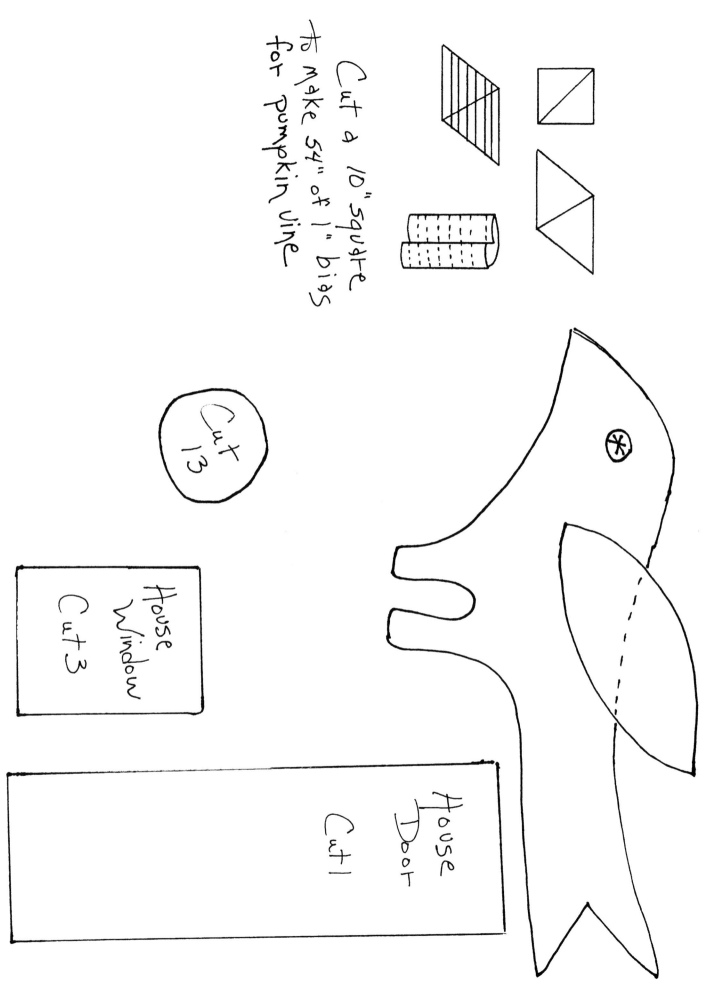

Cut a 10" square
to make 54" of 1" bias
for pumpkin vine

Cut 13

House
Window
Cut 3

House
Door
Cut 1

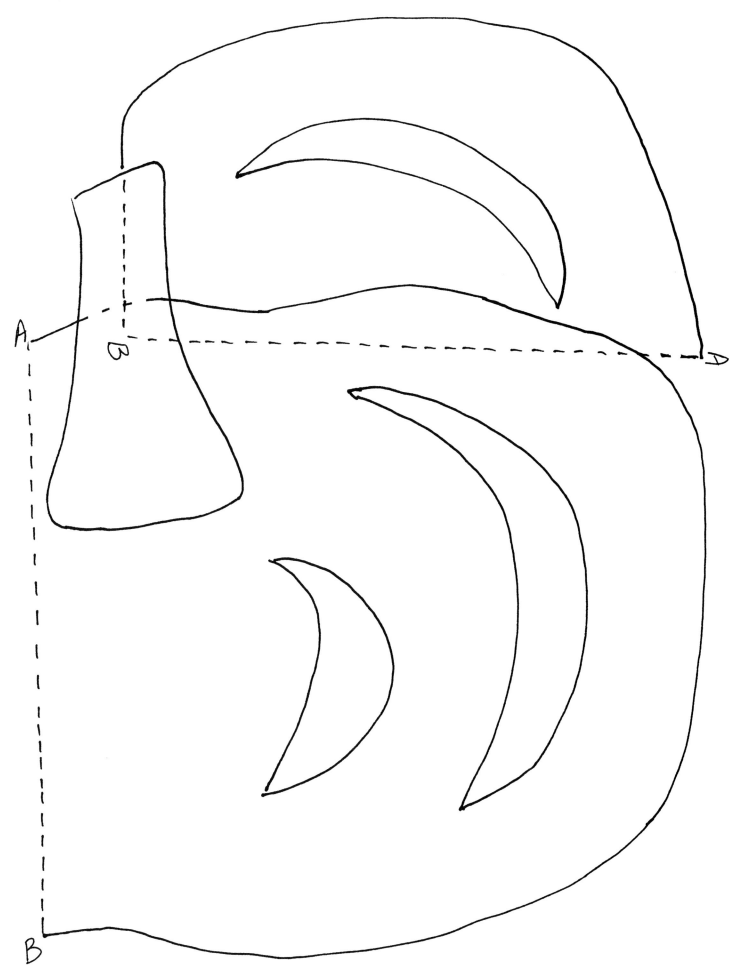

A

B

B

A

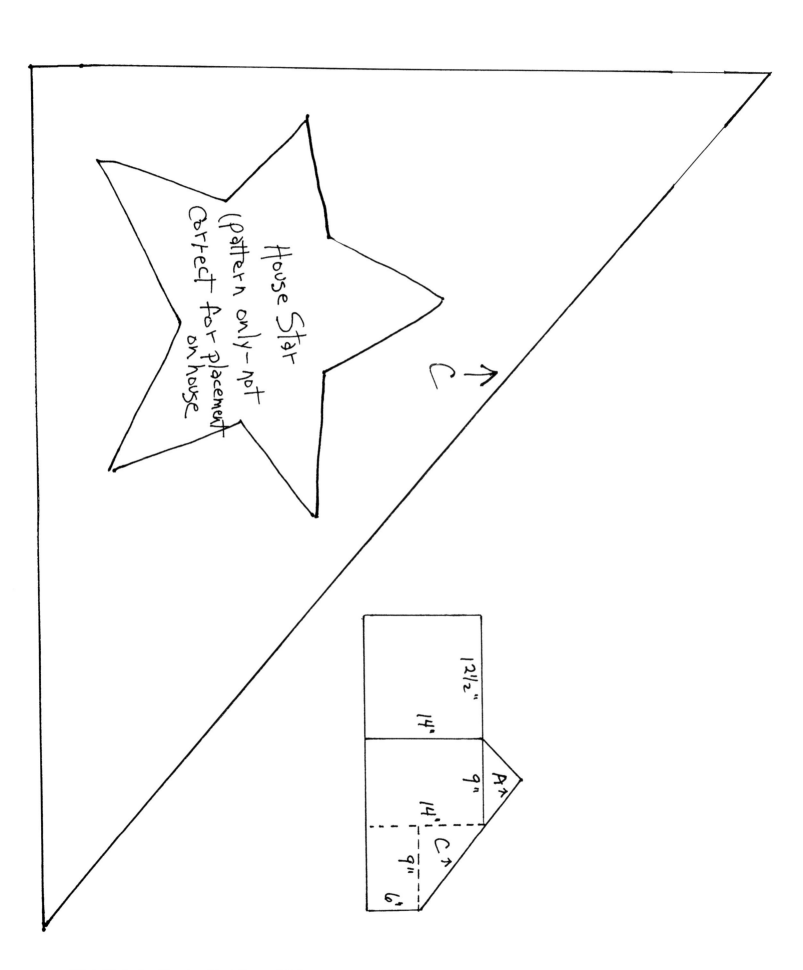

House Star
(pattern only—not
correct for placement
on house)

C →

12½"

14"

A →

9"

14"

C →

9"

6"

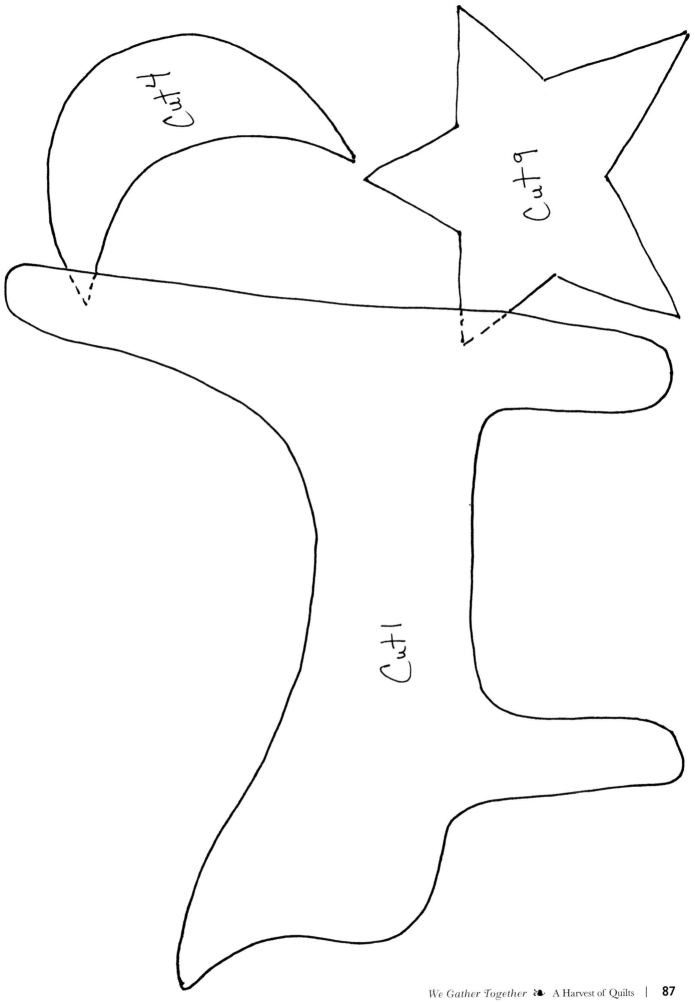

Cut 4

Cut 9

Cut 1

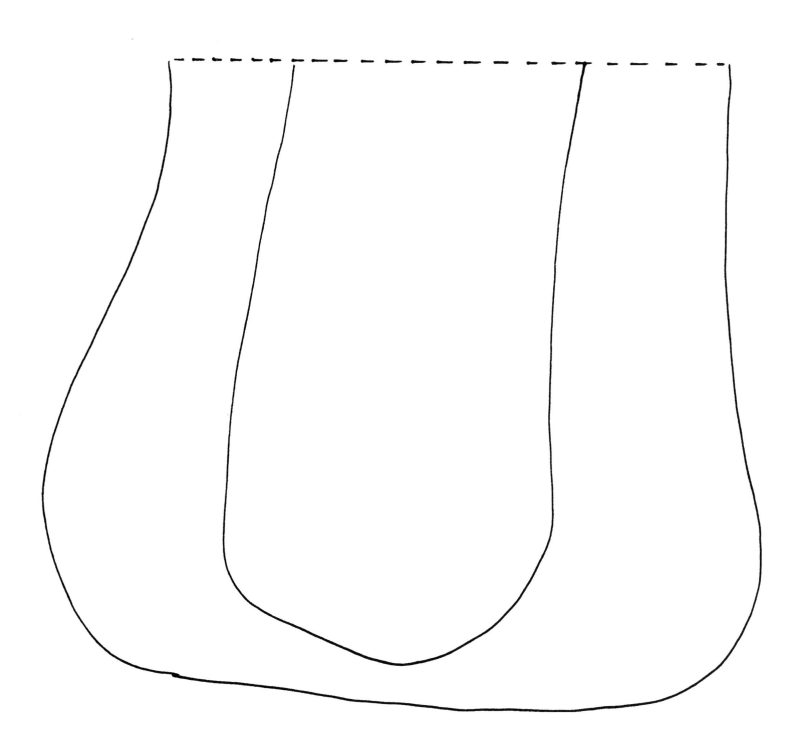

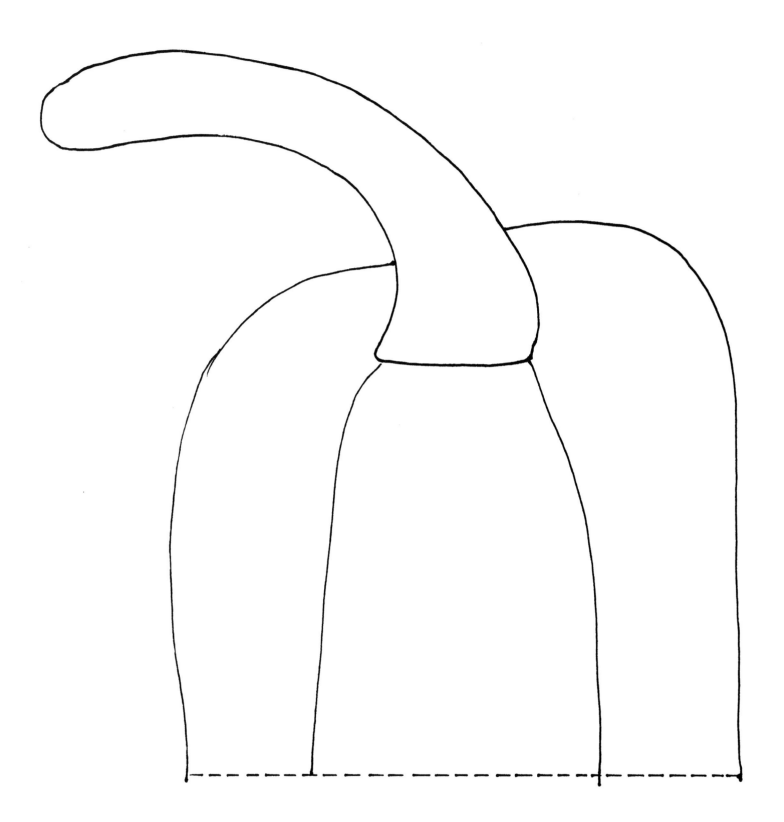

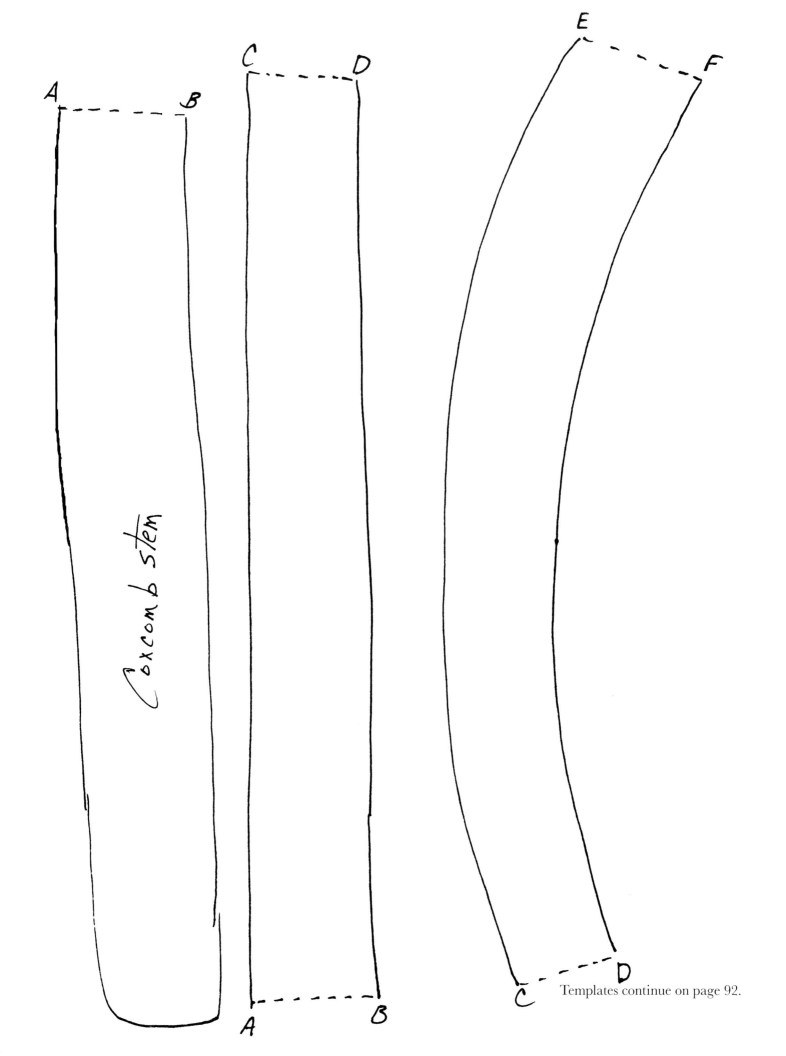

Coxcomb stem

Templates continue on page 92.

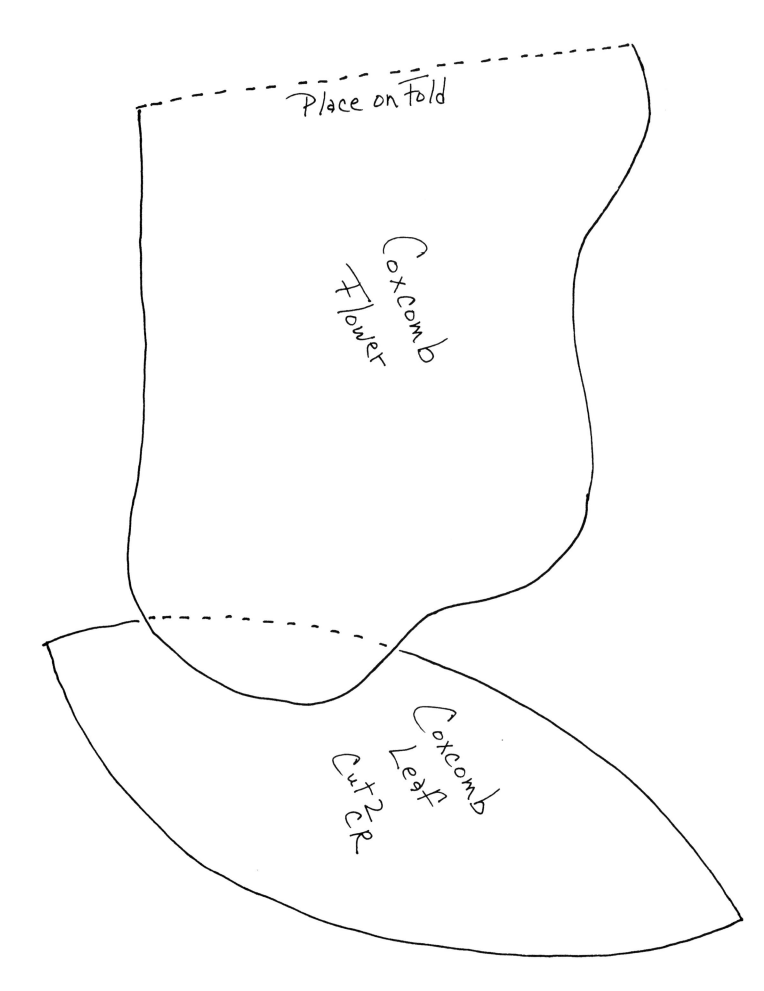

Place on Fold

Coxcomb Flower

Coxcomb Leaf Cut 2 CR

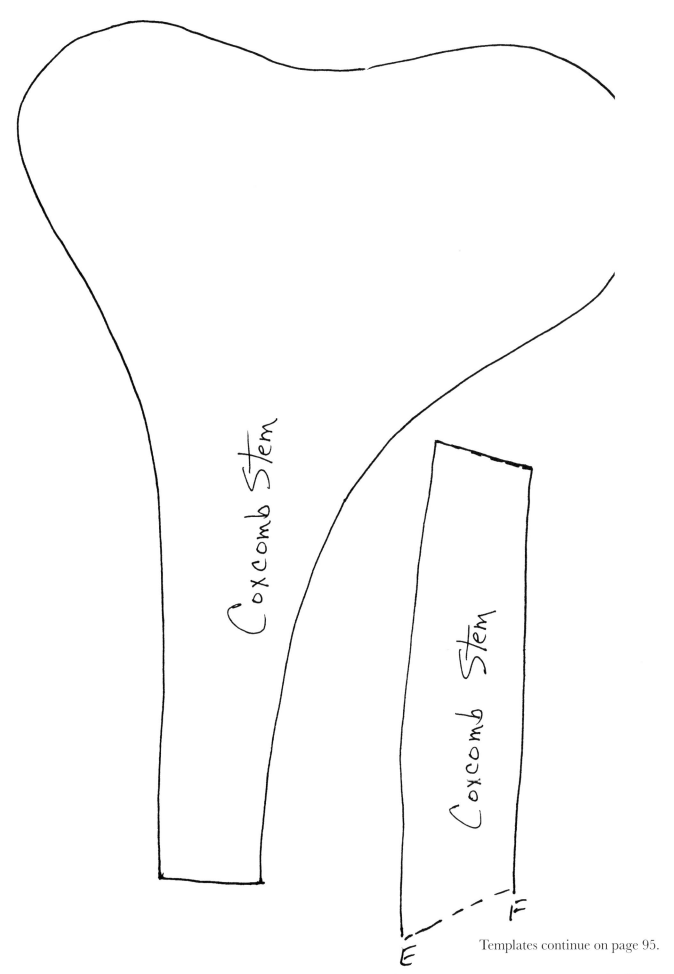

Coxcomb Stem

Coxcomb Stem

E

F

Templates continue on page 95.

Cut 5

Cut 5

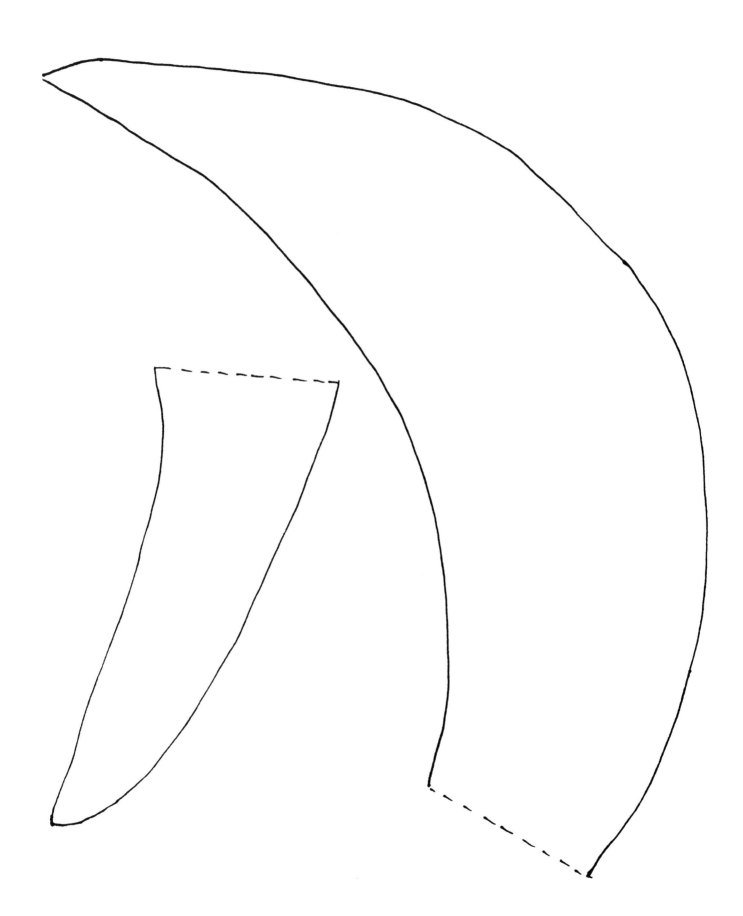

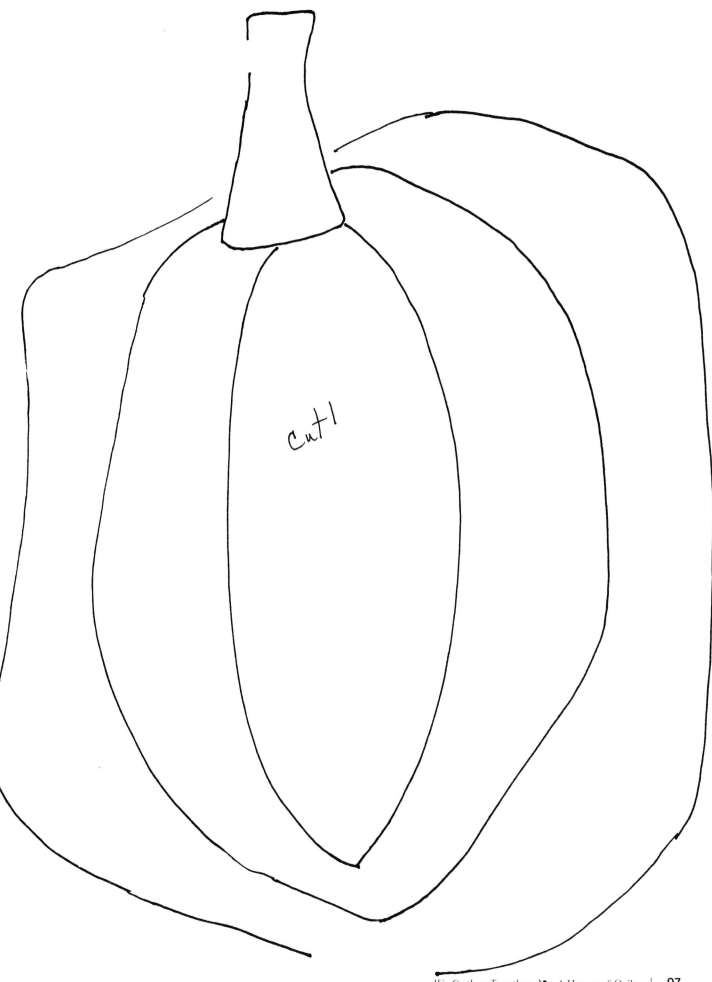

cut 1

Pumpkins, Turkeys and Geese

Size 68" x 70"

Fabric Requirements:

- Turkey backgrounds: 5/8 yard of 3

- Pumpkin backgrounds: Fat quarter of 4 and fat eighth of 1

- Pumpkin #1 (top left): Fat quarter for outer pumpkin, fat eighth for middle and scraps for inner part

- Pumpkin #2 (top right): Fat quarter for pumpkin, scraps for markings

- Pumpkin #3 (middle left): Fat quarter for outer pumpkin, fat eighth for middle

- Pumpkin #4 (middle right): Fat eighth for pumpkin

- Pumpkin #5 (bottom left): Fat eighth for outer pumpkin, fat eighth for middle and scraps for inner part

- Pumpkin #6 (bottom right): Fat quarter for pumpkin, scraps for markings

- All pumpkin stems are scraps from green and brown fabrics

- Turkeys: 3 different fat quarters for bodies and wings, fat eighth for markings. Fat eighth for combs, wattles and feet, 3 star buttons for eyes

- Triangle squares: 1/4 yard each of 7 darks and 7 lights and mediums

- Flying Geese: 1/4 yard of 5 golds. 1/4 yard of first dark, 1/3 yard of second dark and 1/4 yard of 3rd dark

- Strips and Turkey beards: 1/4 yard

- Dark Sashing: 1/4 yard

- Stop Border: 1/2 yard

- Outer Border: 1 3/8 yards

- Binding: 7/8 yard

Instructions:

(These measurements include seam allowance)

- Refer to the diagram and cut the turkey and pumpkin backgrounds. All measurements in the diagram are finished sizes so be sure to add the 1/2" seam allowance to all background blocks.

- Refer to the General Instructions and cut the appliqué shapes from freezer paper.

- Place the shapes on the background. Pin, glue stick or baste the shapes into place on the background. Appliqué in place.

Half-Square Triangles

- There are a total of 66 half-square triangles with 7 color combinations. You will need 7 combinations, each combination having a dark fabric and a light or mediums fabric. Cut and piece 10 - 4" finished half-square triangles of each combination. Use triangle paper or cut 5 - 4 7/8" squares each of light and dark fabrics in each color combination. Cut in half diagonally and sew one light to one dark. Open and press toward the darkest fabric.

Flying Geese Units:

- There are a total of 75 - 2" x 4" finished flying geese units.

- Geese: There are five golds used for the geese.

You will need 15 geese of each gold. Cut 4 - 5 1/4" squares of each gold prints and homespuns. Now cut the squares in quarters diagonally. This will give you 16 geese in each color. Use a rough progression of fabrics as follows, starting from the bottom (I'll give you the fabrics I used to give you the general idea): gold small leaf print, gold star/vine print, gold large leaf and berry print, cream/gold check print, gold stripe homespun.

Geese Backgrounds:

&❧ From left to right of quilt

- Rows One (15) and Four (8) - Cut 23 - 2 7/8" squares of first dark. Cut the squares from corner to corner once on the diagonal and sew a triangle to each side of your goose.

- Rows Two (10) and Six (27): Cut 37 - 2 7/8" squares of second dark.

- Cut the squares from corner to corner once on the diagonal and sew a triangle to each side of your goose.

- Rows Three (11) and Five (4) - Cut 15 - 2 7/8" squares of third dark. Cut the squares from corner to corner once on the diagonal and sew a triangle to each side of your goose.

&❧ Sashing: The 4 1/2" x 2 1/2" strip to the left of Row 3 of the flying geese is cut from a scrap of one of the lights. All other sashing is cut from the dark solid as follows:

- 5 rectangles 2 1/2" x 4 1/2"

- 1 rectangle 2 1/2" x 10 1/2"

- 2 rectangles 2 1/2" x 16 1/2"

- Refer to the diagram for placement.

&❧ Assembly: Sew the pumpkin blocks, turkey blocks, sashing strips, flying geese and half-square triangles together referring to the diagram and photo.

Borders:

&❧ Cut 2 - 56 1/2" x 1 1/2" stop borders and sew to the top and bottom.

&❧ Cut 2 - 60 1/2" x 1 1/2" stop borders and sew to the sides.

&❧ Cut 2 - 60 1/2" x 5 1/2" outer borders and sew to the sides.

&❧ Cut 2 - 68 1/2" x 5 1/2" outer borders and sew to the top and bottom.

&❧ Quilt as desired.

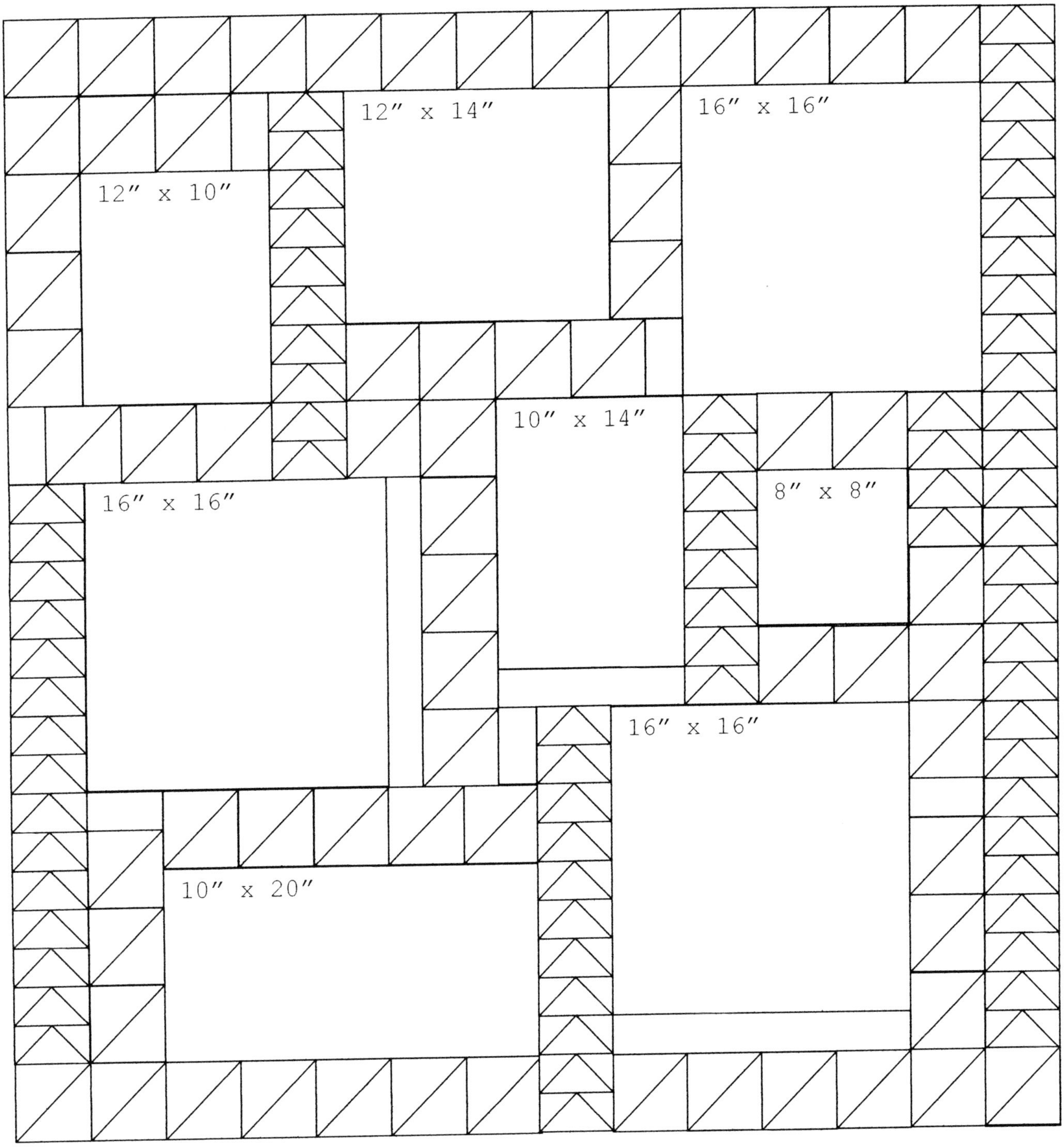

12" x 10"

12" x 14"

16" x 16"

10" x 14"

16" x 16"

8" x 8"

16" x 16"

10" x 20"

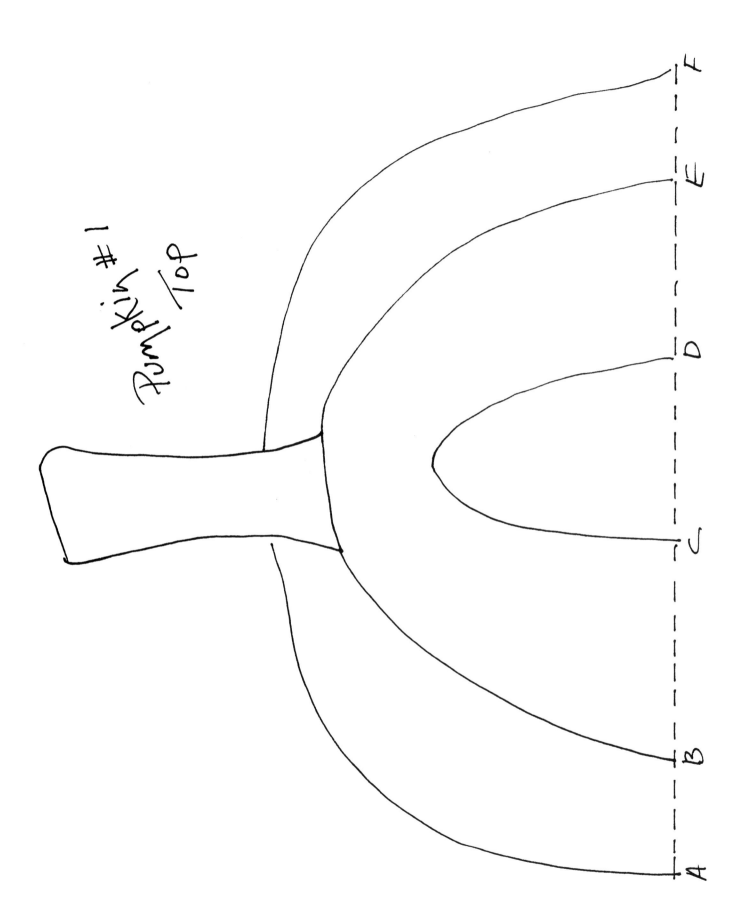

Pumpkin #1
Top

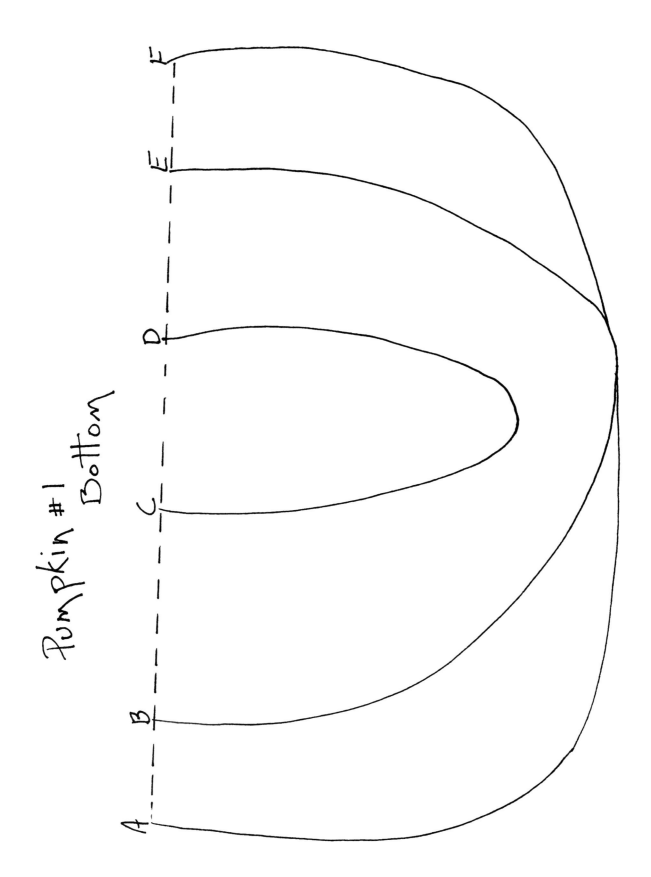

Pumpkin #1
Bottom

A
B
C
D
E
F

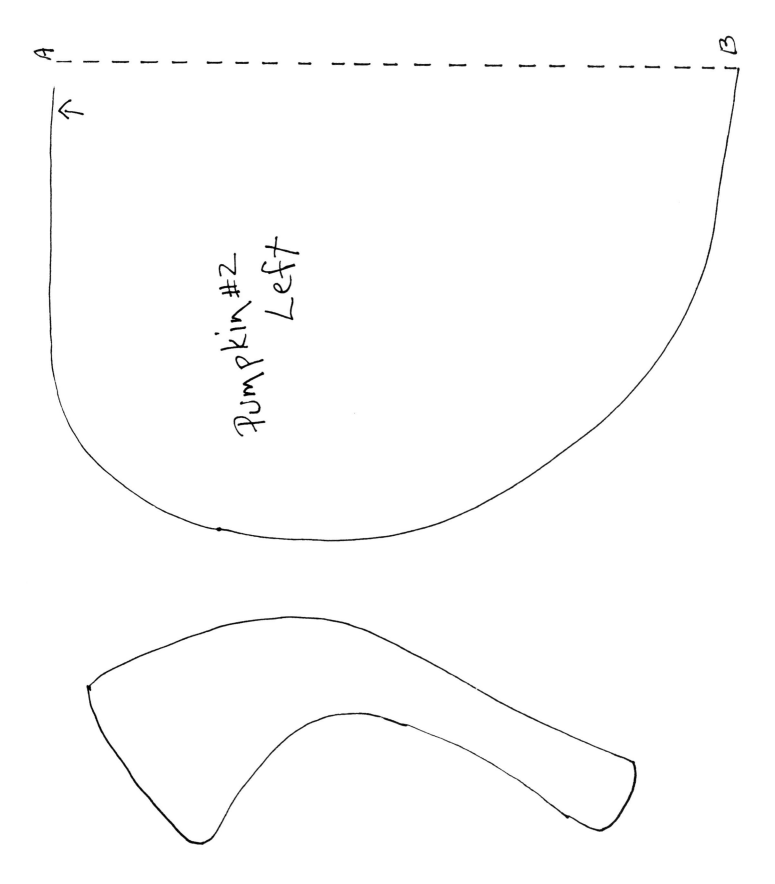

A

B

Pumpkin #2
Left

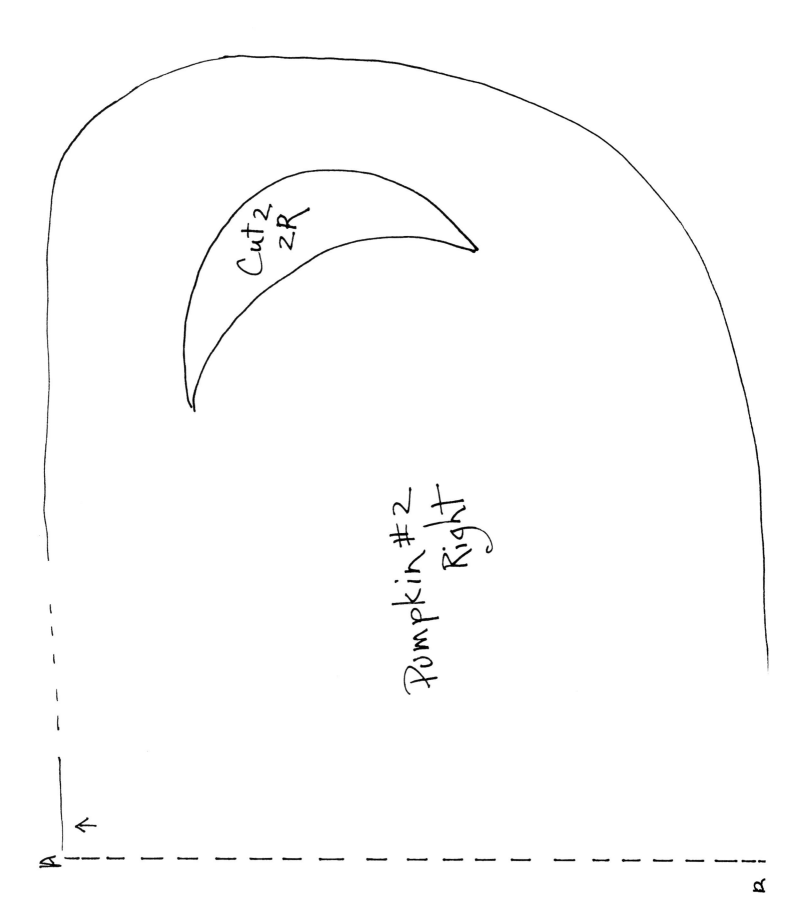

Cut 2
2R

Pumpkin #2
Right

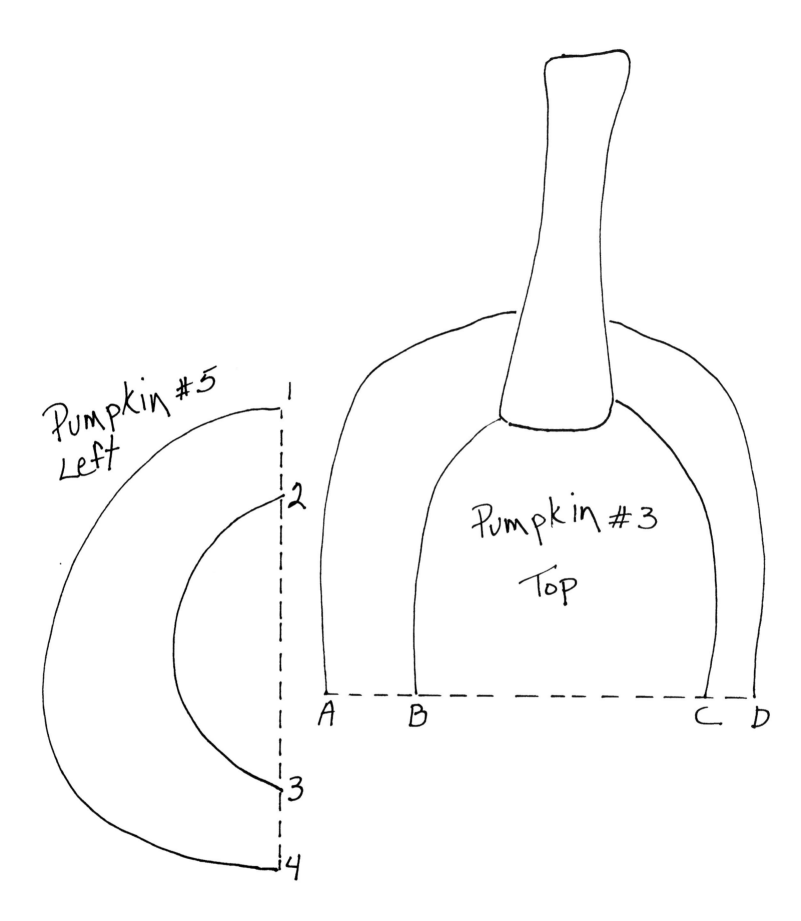

Pumpkin #5
Left

1

2

3

4

Pumpkin #3

Top

A

B

C

D

Templates continue on page 108

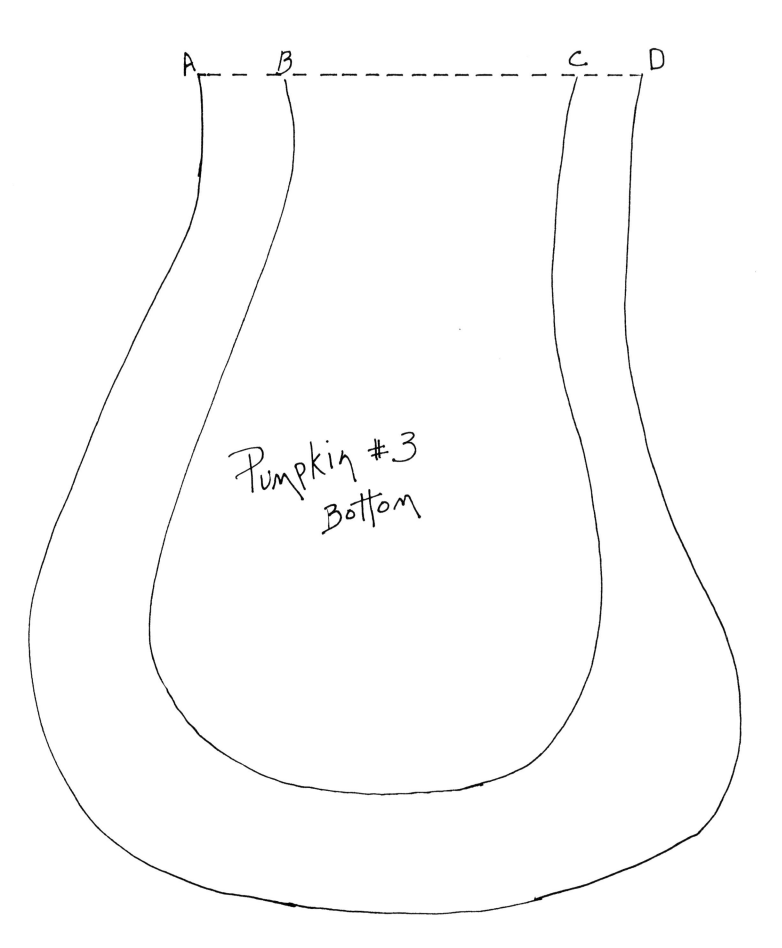

Pumpkin #3
Bottom

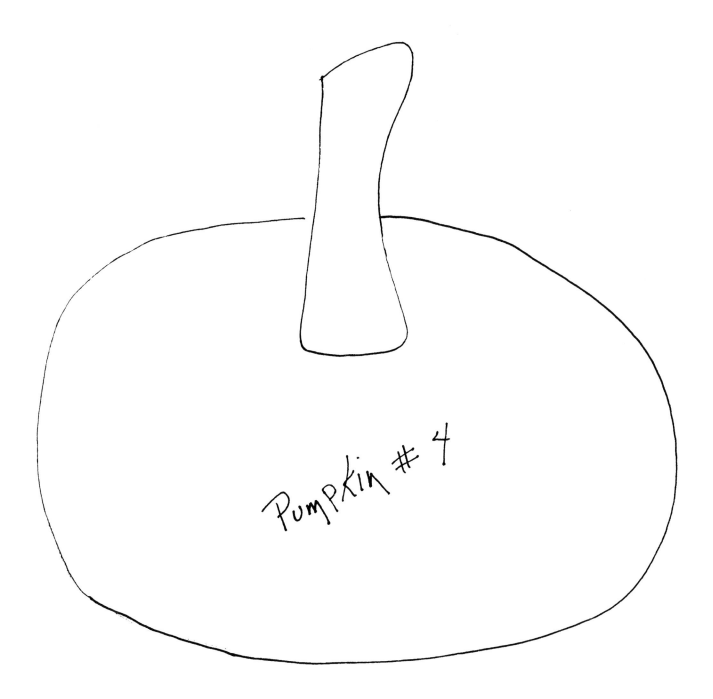

Pumpkin # 4

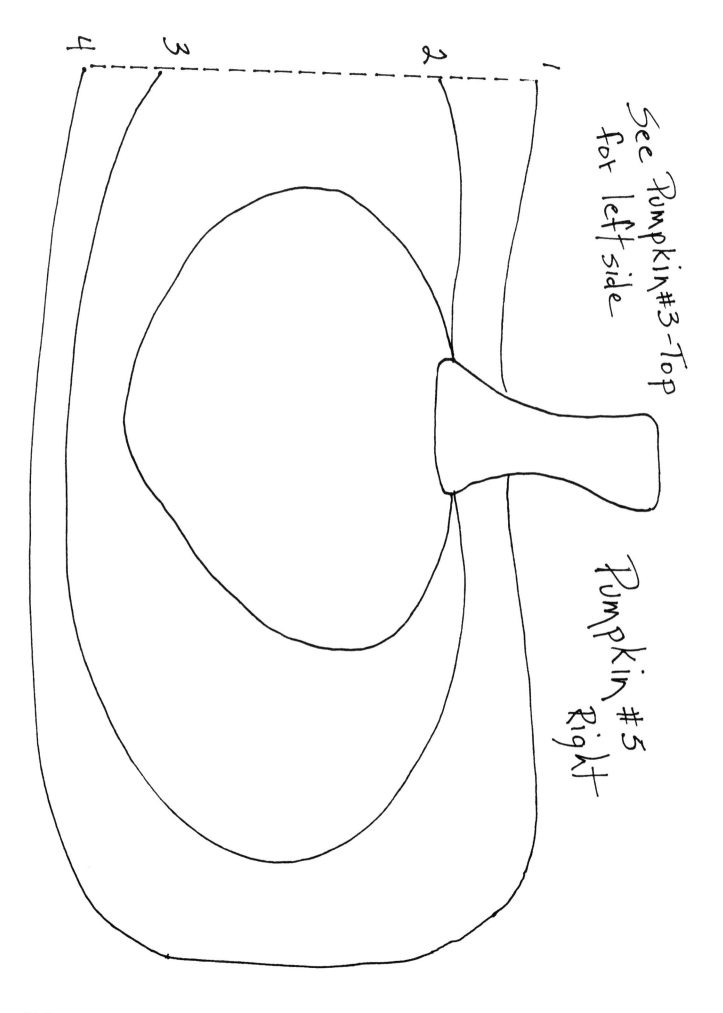

See Pumpkin #3-Top
for left side

Pumpkin #5
Right

4 3 2 1

Pumpkin #6

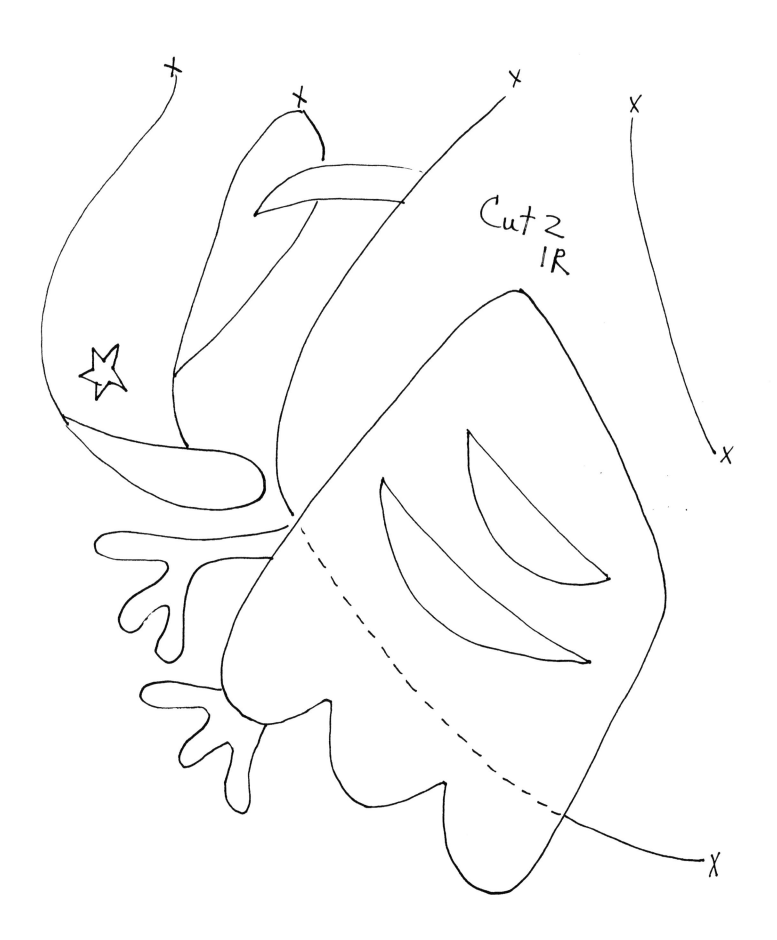

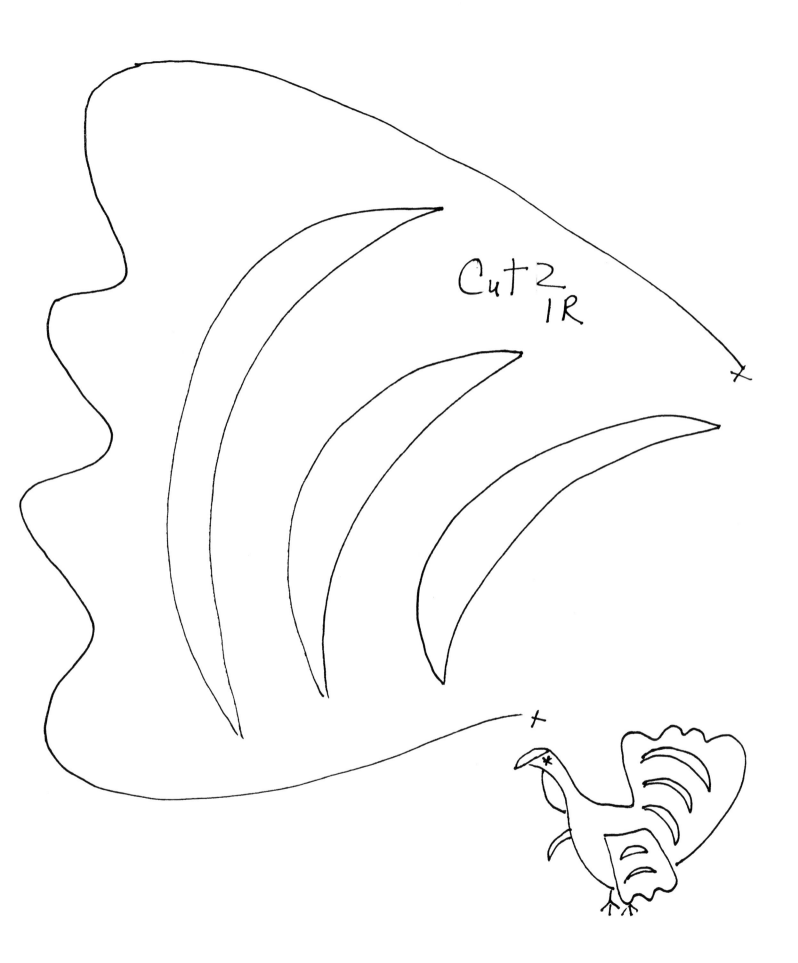

Cut 2
1R

Pumpkin Rug

Size: 16" x 26 1/4"

Requirements:

- 28" x 34" piece of monkscloth, hemmed
- Fat quarter of 2 wools for pumpkins
- 3/4 yard wool for background
- Fat quarter wool for gold sawteeth
- Scraps of assorted colors of wool for stems, pumpkin markings, heart, and star
- 1/8 yard wool for inner border
- 1/2 yard wool for outer border

Mark the center point of the monkscloth from top to bottom and from side to side. From that center point, mark 6" out on the left and 6" out from the right. Draw a line from top to bottom on each side of the monkscloth with a pencil. These will be reference lines.

Now measure 11" from the center point towards the top. Draw a line 11" towards the top joining the two side reference lines. Now measure 11" from the center point toward the bottom. Draw a line 11" toward the bottom joining the two side reference lines. You should now have a 12" x 22" background rectangle. Trace the rectangle lines with a permanent marker using a straight edge ruler or better still, a quilting square.

The half-square triangles are 2" square. Come down from the mark you made at the bottom of the rectangle. Draw 6 - 2" squares. Then draw a diagonal line from corner to corner on each square. You have now marked the bottom border.

Mark 1/4" out from each side line and the top line. Take a look at the photo. You have just marked the inside blue border.

Measure out 2" on the sides and top of the inside blue border. Mark that measurement with a permanent marking pen. That is the outside border.

Trace the pumpkin patterns given on pages 117 – 119.

See the instructions on Marking your Canvas if necessary. After everything is marked, follow the directions below to make this wonderful rug.

Rug Hooking for Quilters

Marking your Canvas:

We use monkscloth for a canvas instead of burlap. It costs more but is a lot easier to hook through. It should be available at your local quilt shop.

Cut a piece of monkscloth about 12" larger than the dimensions of the rug. You should have a 6" space all the way around the edge of the rug. Hem the material immediately as it tends to fray.

With a pencil, draw the background for the rug onto a piece of paper using the dimensions given in the instruction diagram. Tape a couple of pieces of freezer paper together and draw on the side that's not waxy. Draw the pattern pieces on a separate piece of paper and cut them out. You will then be able to move them around on the background until you are satisfied with the placement. Glue or tape them in place. Using a medium-point black permanent marker, go over your pencil lines.

Pin the pattern face down to the wrong side of the monkscloth, making sure it is in the middle. Turn both pieces over. Using a light table or the good old window and light source trick, draw your pattern onto the monkscloth with a medium-point black permanent marker.

Fabric:

Always use good quality 100% wool. Wash all fabric in warm water with detergent.

Hoop or Frame:

It is possible to hook using a wooden hoop with or without a stand. I prefer using a hooking frame which has Velcro-like strips made out of metal on all four sides that holds the monkscloth in place.

Cutting your Wool into Strips:

Most strips for primitive hooking should be cut to a width of 1/4" to 3/8". Several methods can be used. First there are cutters that can be purchased with interchangeable heads to cut wool into different widths. Another method is to use a rotary cutter and a ruler. A third method and the one I prefer is to simply cut the strips with a pair of scissors. The strips will be uneven but this greatly enhances the "primitive" look.

Hooking:

Begin hooking one row in from the outline of the pattern shape. If you hook on the line, you will enlarge your pattern.

If you are right handed, the hook is held in the right hand above the pattern. The wool strip is held in the left hand underneath the pattern. Insert the hook through a hole in the monkscloth, catch the strip of wool with the hook and pull it through. Pull this starting piece about 1/2" above the pattern.

To keep the wool strip straight with no curled edges, pull the loop higher than the 1/4" with the hook, then pull the strip back to the 1/4" height with the left hand. The top pile should be even with the loops lightly touching and no monkscloth should be showing. DO NOT HOOK IN EVERY HOLE! This is called "overhooking" and novice hookers are prone to this mistake. There are three exceptions to this rule:

Hooking on the diagonal.

Beginning and ending strips

Near a corner. Hook a little tighter to secure the corner.

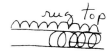

But as a general rule, the loops should be lightly touching, not crammed together.

When you get to the end of a strip of wool, simply pull it through the top of the monkscloth. Start the next strip of wool in the same hole. (Try not to start a new strip when turning a corner.) Your end pieces and beginning pieces will be sticking out of the same hole. After a few more loops, cut them off evenly with the others and they will disappear. Wool strips should never be carried from one row to another. If your strip is too wide for the area you are hooking, simply trim the strip.

Begin hooking as you do quilting, with an object near the center of the pattern. Always outline the object first. Quite often you will use a color that is a bit different rather than matching the piece exactly. This will give you some definition to the object. Fill in the contours. If the object has more than one part, start hooking the center and work outward. If at all possible, do not hook in straight lines. If the object is large, draw imaginary lines with your strips and fill in.

When you appliqué a quilt, you do the background first, then add the objects. Hooking is the other way around. Hook all of the objects in the rug before filling in the background. To hook the background, outline the outside and hook around all the objects for a couple of rows. Then fill in portions of the background as you would a large object. Stay away from rows unless the subject calls for it, for example, a log cabin design. Rows are definitely the exception, not the rule.

Binding your Rug:

For binding your rug, you need two things:

- Wool yarn close to the color of your outside border.

- Binding tape.

- Trim the monkscloth to around 1 1/2" from the edge. Turn the monkscloth back from the edge of your rug. With a large-eye tapestry needle, loop the yarn along the edge touching the loops of wool in the rug. Bury your ends as you go along. We are forming a ridge at the edge of the rug so we can attach the tape. This will keep the monkscloth from showing through.

As you come to each corner, cut a square out of the monkscloth up to within 3/8" of the edge.

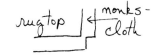

Continue with the yarn until you have a ridge of yarn all the way around the rug. Now sew your binding tape to this ridge and to the rug, either mitering the corners or squaring them.

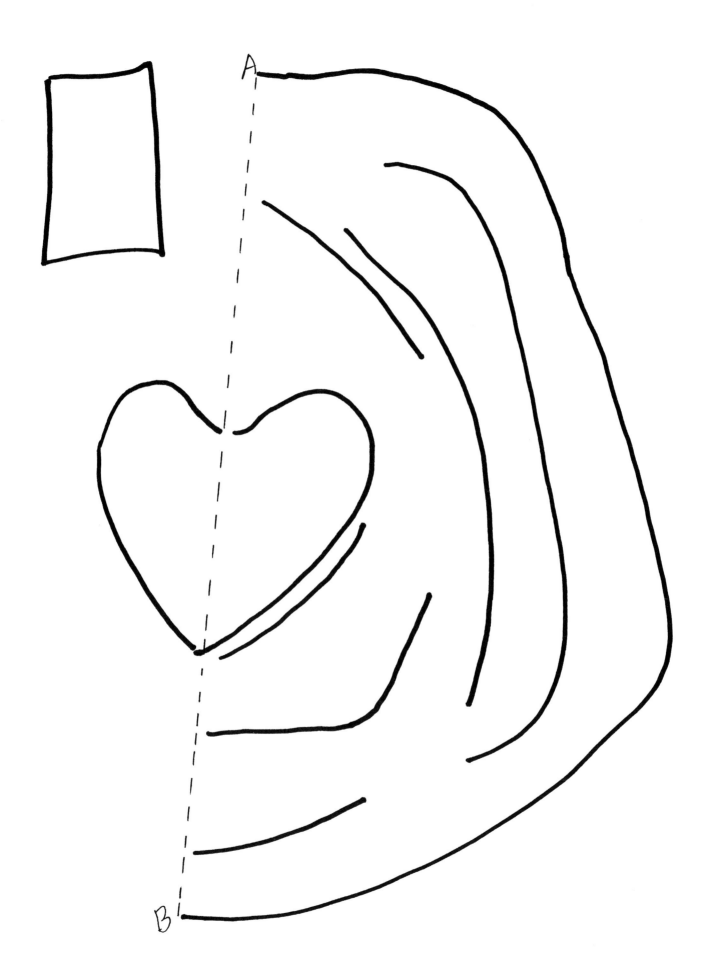

A

B

Other Star Books

One Piece at a Time by Kansas City Star Books – 1999

More Kansas City Star Quilts by Kansas City Star Books – 2000

Outside the Box: Hexagon Patterns from The Kansas City Star by Edie McGinnis – 2001

Prairie Flower: A Year on the Plains by Barbara Brackman – 2001

The Sister Blocks by Edie McGinnis – 2001

Kansas City Quiltmakers by Doug Worgul – 2001

O' Glory: Americana Quilts Blocks from The Kansas City Star by Edie McGinnis – 2001

Hearts and Flowers: Hand Appliqué from Start to Finish by Kathy Delaney – 2002

Roads and Curves Ahead: A Trip Through Time with Classic Kansas City Star *Quilt Blocks* by Edie McGinnis – 2002

Celebration of American Life: Appliqué Patterns Honoring a Nation and Its People by Barb Adams and Alma Allen – 2002

Women of Grace & Charm: A Quilting Tribute to the Women Who Served in World War II by Barb Adams and Alma Allen – 2003

A Heartland Album: More Techniques in Hand Appliqué by Kathy Delaney – 2003

Quilting a Poem: Designs Inspired by America's Poets by Frances Kite and Deb Rowden – 2003

Carolyn's Paper Pieced Garden: Patterns for Miniature and Full-Sized Quilts by Carolyn Cullinan McCormick – 2003

Friendships in Bloom: Round Robin Quilts by Marjorie Nelson and Rebecca Nelson-Zerfas – 2003

Baskets of Treasures: Designs Inspired by Life Along the River by Edie McGinnis – 2003

Heart & Home: Unique American Women and the Houses that Inspire by Kathy Schmitz – 2003

Women of Design: Quilts in the Newspaper by Barbara Brackman – 2004

The Basics: An Easy Guide to Beginning Quiltmaking by Kathy Delaney – 2004

Four Block Quilts: Echoes of History, Pieced Boldly & Appliquéd Freely by Terry Clothier Thompson – 2004

No Boundaries: Bringing Your Fabric Over the Edge by Edie McGinnis – 2004

Horn of Plenty for a New Century by Kathy Delaney – 2004

Quilting the Garden by Barb Adams and Alma Allen – 2004

Stars All Around Us: Quilts and Projects Inspired by a Beloved Symbol by Cherie Ralston – 2005

Quilters' Stories: Collecting History in the Heart of America by Deb Rowden – 2005

Libertyville: Where Liberty Dwells, There is My Country by Terry Clothier Thompson – 2005

Sparkling Jewels, Pearls of Wisdom by Edie McGinnis – 2005

Grapefruit Juice and Sugar: Bold Quilts Inspired by Grandmother's Legacy by Jenifer Dick – 2005

Home Sweet Home by Barb Adams and Alma Allen – 2005

Patterns of History: The Challenge Winners by Kathy Delaney – 2005

My Quilt Stories by Debra Rowden – 2005

Quilts in Red and Green and the Women Who Made Them by Nancy Hornback and Terry Clothier Thompson – 2006

Hard Times, Splendid Quilts: A 1930s Celebration, Paper Piecing from The Kansas City Star by Carolyn Cullinan McCormick – 2006

Art Nouveau Quilts for the 21st Century by Bea Oglesby – 2006

Designer Quilts: Great Projects from Moda's Best Fabric Artists – 2006

Birds of a Feather by Barb Adams and Alma Allen – 2006

Feedsacks! Beautiful Quilts from Humble Beginnings by Edie McGinnis – 2006

Kansas Spirit: Historical Quilt Blocks and the Saga of the Sunflower State by Jeanne Poore – 2006

Bold Improvisation: Searching for African-American Quilts – The Heffley Collection by Scott Heffley – 2007

The Soulful Art of African-American Quilts: Nineteen Bold, Improvisational Projects by Sonie Ruffin – 2007

Alphabet Quilts: Letters for All Ages by Bea Oglesby – 2007

Beyond the Basics: A Potpourri of Quiltmaking Techniques by Kathy Delaney – 2007

Golden's Journal: 20 Sampler Blocks Honoring Prairie Farm Life by Christina DeArmond, Eula Lang and Kaye Spitzli – 2007

Borderland in Butternut and Blue: A Sampler Quilt to Recall the Civil War Along the Kansas/Missouri Border by Barbara Brackman – 2007

Come to the Fair: Quilts that Celebrate State Fair Traditions by Edie McGinnis – 2007

Cotton and Wool: Miss Jump's Farewell by Linda Brannock – 2007

You're Invited! Quilts and Homes to Inspire by Barb Adams and Alma Allen, Blackbird Designs – 2007

Portable Patchwork: Who Says You Can't Take it With You? by Donna Thomas – 2008

Quilts for Rosie: Paper Piecing Patterns from the '40s by Carolyn Cullinan McCormick – 2008

Fruit Salad: Appliqué Designs for Delicious Quilts by Bea Oglesby – 2008

Red, Green and Beyond by Nancy Hornback and Terry Clothier Thompson – 2008

A Dusty Garden Grows by Terry Clothier Thompson – 2008

We Gather Together: A Harvest of Quilts by Jan Patek – 2008

With These Hands: 19th Century-Inspired Primitive Projects for Your Home by Maggie Bonanomi – 2008

Queen Bees Mysteries:
Murders on Elderberry Road by Sally Goldenbaum – 2003

A Murder of Taste by Sally Goldenbaum – 2004

Murder on a Starry Night by Sally Goldenbaum – 2005

Dog-Gone Murder by Marnette Falley – 2008

Project Books:
Fan Quilt Memories by Jeanne Poore – 2000

Santa's Parade of Nursery Rhymes by Jeanne Poore – 2001

As the Crow Flies by Edie McGinnis – 2007

Sweet Inspirations by Pam Manning – 2007

Quilts Through the Camera's Eye by Terry Clothier Thompson – 2007

Louisa May Alcott: Quilts of Her Life, Her Work, Her Heart by Terry Clothier Thompson – 2008

The Lincoln Museum Quilt: A Reproduction for Abe's Frontier Cabin by Barbara Brackman and Deb Rowden – 2008

Dinosaurs - Stomp, Chomp and Roar by Pam Manning - 2008

Notes:

Notes:

Notes: